Ecosystem
Science Fair Projects

Library of Congress Cataloging-in-Publication Data

Walker, Pam, 1958–
 Ecosystem science fair projects, revised and expanded using the scientific method /
Pam Walker and Elaine Wood.
     p. cm. — (Biology science projects using the scientific method)
 Summary: "Explains how to use the scientific method to conduct several science
experiments about ecosystems. Includes ideas for science fair projects"—Provided by publisher.
 Includes bibliographical references and index.
 ISBN 978-0-7660-3419-8
 1. Ecology projects—Juvenile literature. 2. Ecology—Experiments—Juvenile literature.
I. Wood, Elaine, 1950– II. Title.
 QH541.24.W348 2010
 577.078—dc22
                            2009019375

Printed in the United States of America

092009 Lake Book Manufacturing, Inc., Melrose Park, IL

10 9 8 7 6 5 4 3 2 1

To Our Readers: We have done our best to make sure all Internet Addresses in this book
were active and appropriate when we went to press. However, the author and the publisher
have no control over and assume no liability for the material available on those Internet sites
or on other Web sites they may link to. Any comments or suggestions can be sent by e-mail
to comments@enslow.com or to the address on the back cover.

♻ Enslow Publishers, Inc. is committed to printing our books on recycled paper. The paper in
every book contains between 10% to 30% post-consumer waste (PCW). The cover board on the
outside of each book contains 100% PCW. Our goal is to do our part to help young people and
the environment too!

Illustration Credits: Tom LaBaff and Stephanie LaBaff

Editorial Revision: Lily Book Productions

Design: Oxygen Design

Photo Credits: Shutterstock, pp. 3, 6, 26, 43, 56, 58, 75, 80, 84, 86, 99, 104, 111, 116.

Cover Photos: Shutterstock

Revised Edition of *Ecosystem Science Fair Projects Using Worms, Leaves, Crickets,
and Other Stuff*, Copyright © 2005.

Biology Science Projects
Using the Scientific Method

Ecosystem
Science Fair Projects

Revised and Expanded
Using the Scientific Method

Pam Walker
and Elaine Wood

Enslow Publishers, Inc.
40 Industrial Road
Box 398
Berkeley Heights, NJ 07922
USA

http://www.enslow.com

Contents

Introduction: Ecosystem Experiments and Projects Using the Scientific Method 7

How Scientists Search for Answers 10

Using the Scientific Method
in Experiments and Projects 12

Science Fairs 20

Safety First 24

1 Ecosystems 27

1.1 Living on the Edge 30

1.2 The Climate Suits Me 35

1.3 In the Dark 39

1.4 My Plot or Yours? 45

1.5 Soil Survivors 51

2 Nonliving Factors Affect Ecosystems 59

2.1 Thirsty Little Sprouts 61

2.2 A Drop in the Bag 65

2.3 Fermentation Factories 70

2.4 Cool Fish 76

2.5 The Right Light 81

3 Living Factors Affect Ecosystems 87

3.1 Give Me Space 90

3.2 Pesky Plants! 95

3.3 Out of Sight 100

3.4 Too Close for Comfort 106

3.5 It's a Gas 112

4 Humans Affect Ecosystems 117

4.1 Probing Pollution 120

4.2 No Salt, Please 125

4.3 Acid Bath 131

4.4 Shrimp Forecast:
Clear to Partly Cloudy 136

4.5 Packed Tight 142

Appendix: Science Supply Companies 148

Glossary 149

Further Reading 154

Internet Addresses 155

Index 156

Indicates experiments that contain Science Project Ideas.

INTRODUCTION

Ecosystem Experiments and Projects Using the Scientific Method

If you take a stroll through your neighborhood, what parts of the natural world do you see? Are plants growing? Can you spot birds flying overhead, or glimpse any insects on the ground? In the place where you live, is the weather warm or cold? The animals, plants, and temperature are just a few of the many parts of your ecosystem. An ecosystem is made up of the living things in an area along with the nonliving factors in that environment.

A science project is an ideal way for you to launch your own exploration of ecosystems and do some real science. Science projects provide great

◀ A snowy owl stands on the frozen ice of the Hudson River. The animals, plants, and environment of an area make up its ecosystem.

learning experiences, plus they give you a chance to find out more about a topic that interests you.

Science projects also help you see that science is not just a collection of facts that must be studied or memorized. Science is an active, ongoing process. When you get involved in a science project, you do a lot of thinking and ask lots of questions. In science, you will make decisions, create workable plans, and carry them out. As you read this book, your experiments will show how ecosystems work and why they are important. Let's begin our journey!

Experiments and Projects

This book contains lots of fun experiments about ecosystems. You'll also be given suggestions for independent investigations that you can do yourself. Many of the experiments are followed by a section called Science Project Ideas. This section contains great ideas for your own science fair projects.

To do some of the projects in this book, you may need people to help you, because more than one pair of hands may be required. Try to choose helpers who are patient and who enjoy experimenting as much as you do.

The experiments are all easy to do and safe to carry out when the instructions are followed as given. Consult with your school science teacher or some **other responsible adult** to obtain approval before starting any experiments of your own.

If any danger is involved in doing an experiment, it will be made known to you. In some cases, to avoid any danger to you,

you'll be asked to work with **an adult**. Please do so. We don't want you to take any chances that could lead to an injury.

Most of the materials you'll need to carry out the projects and experiments described in this book can be found in your home. Several of the experiments may require items that you can buy from a supermarket, a hobby or toy shop, a hardware store, or one of the science supply companies listed in the appendix. As you begin to use this book, show it to one of the science teachers in your school. Perhaps the teacher will allow you and some of your friends to use the school's equipment.

As you do these projects, you will find it useful to record your ideas, notes, data, and anything else you can conclude from your experiments in a notebook. That way you can keep track of the information you gather and the conclusions you reach. It will also allow you to refer to other experiments you've done that may be useful to you in later projects.

How Scientists
Search for Answers

When scientists have a question to answer, they start by researching. They read scientific literature and consult online science databases that are maintained by universities, research centers, or the government. There, they can study abstracts—summaries of reports—by scientists who have conducted experiments or done similar research in the field.

In this way, they find out whether other scientists have examined the same question or have tried to answer it by doing an experiment. Careful research will tell what kind of experiments, if any, have been done to try to answer the question.

Scientists don't want to repeat experiments that have known and accepted outcomes. Also, they want to avoid repeating any mistakes others may have made while doing similar experiments. If no one else has done scientific work that answers the question, scientists then do further research on how best to do the experiment.

While researching for the experiment, the scientist tries to guess—or predict—the possible results. This prediction is called a hypothesis.

The scientist hopes that a well-researched and carefully planned experiment will prove the hypothesis to be true. At times, however, the results of even the best-planned experiment can be far different from what the scientist expected. Yet even if the results indicate the hypothesis was not true, this does not mean the experiment was a failure. In fact, unexpected results can provide valuable information that leads to a different answer or to another, even better, experiment.

Using the Scientific Method in Experiments and Projects

The Scientific Method

A scientific experiment starts when someone wonders what would happen if certain conditions were set up and tested by following a specific process. In other cases, scientists must observe conditions that already exist. For example, in an experiment testing how environmental conditions may affect an animal population, you can ask the question: "Are the sizes of ant populations in the local forest ecosystems related to the amount of moisture in the soil?"

A hypothesis must be a statement because it has to be proved or disproved. The hypothesis might be:

✓ Large populations of ants are found in very moist soil.

✓ Moisture does not affect the number of ants living in a forest ecosystem.

✓ Ants prefer dry soil.

Next, decide how you are going to do your project. Would you try to count the ants in different areas of the forest? Would you count them all, or just a sample? What criteria would you use to decide how much moisture the soil is holding? How will you measure the moisture?

Before you begin your experiment, decide when you will collect data and for how long. For example, in an experiment on ants and soil moisture, you might want to count ants daily for a period of two weeks. Once you have an idea of the scope of your experiment, develop a data table in your science notebook. This is a place where you can record information as the experiment progresses.

After you have collected your data, you must examine it and decide what it means. This is the time when you will find the answers to your initial questions. You might conclude that there were more ants in the dry part of the forest than in the wet section. When you have your data and conclusions, share them with other people.

Scientists may develop logical explanations for the results of their experiments. These explanations, or theories, then must be tested by more experiments. If the resulting data from more experiments provide compelling support for a theory, then that theory could be accepted by the world of science. But scientists are careful about accepting new theories. If the resulting data contradict a theory, then the theory must be discarded, altered, or retested. That is the scientific method.

Basic Steps in the Scientific Method

The best experiments and science projects usually follow the scientific method's basic steps:

✓ Ask questions about what would happen if certain conditions or events were set up and tested in an experiment.

✓ Do background research to investigate the subject of your questions until you have a main question.

✓ Construct a hypothesis—an answer to your question—that you can then test and investigate with an experiment.

✓ Design and conduct an experiment to test your hypothesis.

✓ Keep records, collecting data, and then analyze what you've recorded.

✓ Draw a conclusion based on the experiment and the data you've recorded.

✓ Write a report about your results.

Your Hypothesis

In this book's experiment, "The Right Light," the question is: "How do differences in light intensity affect the behavior of earthworms?" How do you search for an answer? For your hypothesis? First, you should observe earthworms in their natural environment. What environments do earthworms prefer? How do earthworms behave in light?

After your research, you might make an educated guess in answer to the question; this is your hypothesis: "Earthworms prefer environments away from direct light."

Each experiment in this book has a question and a possible hypothesis. (Remember, this is just one idea for a hypothesis. You may have other ideas!)

Remember: To give your experiment or project every chance of success, prepare a hypothesis that is clear and brief. The simpler the better.

Designing the Experiment

Your experiment will be structured to investigate whether the hypothesis is true or false. The experiment is intended to test the hypothesis, not necessarily to prove that the hypothesis is right.

The results of a well-designed experiment are more valuable than the results of an experiment that is intentionally designed to give the answer you want. The conditions you set up in your experiment must be a fair test of your hypothesis. For example, in the ant population experiment you should get data from several populations. The ant populations should be observed at the same time of day. The populations should also be near a similar amount and type of vegetation.

By carefully carrying out your experiment you'll discover useful information that can be recorded as data. It's most important that the experiment's procedures and results are as accurate as possible. Design the experiment for observable, measurable results. And keep it simple, because the more complicated your experiment is, the more chance you have for error.

Also, if you have friends helping you with an experiment or project, make sure from the start that they'll take their tasks seriously.

Recording Data

Your hypothesis, procedure, data, and conclusions should be recorded immediately as you experiment, but don't keep this information on loose scraps of paper. Record your data in a notebook or logbook—one you use just for experiments. Your notebook should be bound so that you have a permanent record. The laboratory notebook is an essential part of all academic and scientific research.

Make sure to include the date, experiment number, and a brief description of how you collected the data. Write clearly. If you have to cross something out, do it with just a single line, then rewrite the correct information.

Repeat your experiment several times to be sure your results are consistent and your data are trustworthy. Don't try to interpret data as you go along. It's better first to record results accurately, then study them later.

You might even find that you want to replace your experiment's original question with a new one. For example, by answering the question, "What type of shelter best protects an animal from extreme cold?" you learn that animals that live in very cold environments have other adaptations that help them survive in extreme cold. This brings up other questions: "Could animals survive without shelter in the tundra? What adaptations are best suited for the cold weather? Do animals that live in the tundra migrate during the colder winter months?"

Writing the Science Fair Report

Communicate the results of your experiment by writing a clear report. Even the most successful experiment loses its value if the scientist cannot clearly tell what happened. Your report should describe how the experiment was designed and conducted and should state its precise results.

Following are the parts of a science fair report, in the order they should appear:

• The Title Page

The title of your experiment should be centered and near the top of the page. Your teacher will tell you what other information is needed, such as your name, grade, and the name of your science teacher.

• Table of Contents

On the report's second page, list the remaining parts of the report and their page numbers.

• Abstract

Give a brief overview of your experiment. In just a few sentences, tell the purpose of the experiment, what you did, and what you found out. Always write in plain, clear language.

• Introduction

State your hypothesis and explain how you came up with it. Discuss your experiment's main question and how your research led to the hypothesis. Tell what you hoped to achieve when you started the experiment.

• Experiment and Data

This is a detailed step-by-step explanation of how you organized and carried out the experiment. Explain what methods you followed and what materials and equipment you used.

State when the experiment was done (the date and perhaps the time of day) and under what conditions (in a laboratory, outside on a windy day, in cold or warm weather, etc.). Tell who was involved and what part they played in the experiment.

Include clearly labeled graphs and tables of data from the experiment as well as any photographs or drawings that help illustrate your work. Anyone who reads your report should be able to repeat the experiment just the way you did it. (Repeating an experiment is a good way to test whether the original results were obtained correctly.)

Remember: Scientists around the world always use metric measurements in their experiments and projects, and so should you. Use metric liquid and dry measures and a Celsius thermometer.

• Discussion

Explain your results and conclusions, perhaps comparing them with published scientific data you first read about in your research. Consider how the experiment's results relate to your hypothesis. Ask yourself: Do my results support or contradict my hypothesis? Then analyze the answer.

Would you do anything differently if you did this experiment again? State what you've learned as a result of the experiment.

Analyze how your tools and equipment did their tasks, and how well you and others used those tools. If you think the experiment could be done better if designed another way or if you've another hypothesis that might be tested, then include this in your discussion.

• Conclusion
Make a brief summary of your experiment's results. Include only information and data already stated in the report, and be sure not to bring in any new information.

• Acknowledgments
Give credit to everyone who helped you with the experiment. State the names of these individuals and briefly explain who they are and how they assisted you.

• References / Bibliography
List any books, magazines, journals, articles, Web sites, scientific databases, and interviews that were important to your research for the experiment.

Science Fairs

Some of the experiments in this book are followed by a section called Science Project Ideas. These ideas may be appropriate for a science fair. However, judges at science fairs do not reward projects or experiments that are simply copied from a book. For example, a model of your local ecosystem would not impress judges. Data from experiments showing how songbirds in your neighborhood gather materials for their nests would receive far more consideration.

Science fair judges tend to reward creative thought and imagination. However, it is difficult to be creative or imaginative unless you are really interested in your project, so choose something that appeals to you. Consider, too, your own ability and the cost of materials needed for the project.

If you decide to use a project found in this book for a science fair, you will need to find ways to modify or extend it. This should not be difficult because as you do these projects you will think of new ideas for experiments. It is these new

experiments that will make excellent science fair projects because they spring from your own mind and are interesting to you.

If you decide to enter a science fair and have never done so before, you should read some of the books listed in the further reading section. The references that deal specifically with science fairs will provide plenty of helpful hints and lots of useful information that will enable you to avoid the pitfalls that sometimes plague first-time entrants. You will learn how to prepare appealing reports that include charts and graphs, how to set up and display your work, how to present your project, and how to talk to judges and visitors.

Following are some suggestions to consider.

Some Tips for Success at a Science Fair

Science teachers and science fair judges have many different opinions on what makes a good science fair project or experiment. Here are the most important elements:

Originality of Concept is one of the most important things judges consider. Some judges believe that the best science fair projects answer a question that is not found in a science textbook.

Scientific Content is another main area of evaluation. How was science applied in the procedure? Are there sufficient data? Did you stick to your intended procedure and keep good records?

Thoroughness is next in importance. Was the experiment repeated as often as needed to test your hypothesis? Is your notebook complete, and are the data accurate? Does your research bibliography show you did enough library work?

Clarity in how you present your exhibit shows you had a good understanding of the subject you worked on. It's important that your exhibit clearly presents the results of your work.

Effective Process: Judges recognize that how skillfully you carry out a science fair project is usually more important than its results. A well-done project gives students the best understanding of what scientists actually do day-to-day.

Other points to consider when preparing for your science fair:

The Abstract: Write up a brief explanation of your project and make copies for visitors or judges who want to read it.

Knowledge: Be ready to answer questions from visitors and judges confidently. Know what is in your notebook and make some notes on index cards to remind you of important points.

Practice: Before the science fair begins, prepare a list of several questions you think you might be asked. Think about the answers and about how your display can help to support them. Have a friend or parent ask you questions and answer them out loud. Knowing your work thoroughly helps you feel more confident when you're asked about it.

Appearance: Dress and act in a way that shows you take your project seriously. Visitors and judges should get the impression that you're interested in the project and take pride in answering their questions about it.

Remember: Don't block your exhibit. Stand to the side when someone is looking at it.

Your observations need to be displayed for the judges. Photograph the area you are investigating. If you are studying animals or plants that are part of an ecosystem, display photographs of those as well. You will certainly have data from your observations. Record your data in a clear and easy-to-read chart or graph. Be inventive about different ways of showing what you observed.

Safety First

M ost of the projects included in this book are perfectly safe, but it's your responsibility to do them only as directed. Some experiments can be dangerous unless certain precautions are taken. The precautions necessary to prevent accidents and to make the experiments safe and enjoyable are easy to follow.

✔ Do any experiments or projects, whether from this book or of your own design, under the supervision of a science teacher or other knowledgeable adult.

✔ If you need to use a sharp knife or a chemical, get an adult to help you. Do not try to manage these kinds of materials by yourself.

✔ Read all instructions carefully before proceeding with a project. If you have questions, check with your supervisor before going any further.

✔ Maintain a serious attitude while conducting experiments. Fooling around can be dangerous to you and to others.

✔ Never touch a plant if you think it might be poisonous. If necessary, consult a field guide or ask an adult.

✔ Always go to outdoor areas with an adult.

✔ The liquid in some thermometers is mercury. It is dangerous to touch mercury or to breathe mercury vapor, and such thermometers have been banned in many states. When doing these experiments, use only non-mercury thermometers, such as those filled with alcohol. If you have a mercury thermometer in the house, ask an adult if it can be taken to a local mercury thermometer exchange location.

✔ Always return the living things you have collected to the ecosystems from which they came. True scientists have respect for living things.

✔ Read all the way through an experiment before you attempt it. Always have your materials set up before you begin.

✔ Do not eat or drink during an experiment.

And now, on to the experiments!

CHAPTER 1

Ecosystems

You do not have to sign in, register, or pay dues to be a member of nature's biggest organization—an ecosystem. Like everything else that is alive, you already belong. An ecosystem is made up of living things, such as plants, animals, and microorganisms, and nonliving things, such as water, light, and climate. Ecosystems come in many varieties and sizes; they can be as small and wet as a pond or as extensive and dry as a desert.

Ecology takes a close look at what is in an ecosystem, as well as what goes on there. Ecologists call a large group of the same kind of organisms a population. For example, a forest ecosystem might contain several different populations, including a population of long-leaf pine trees, one of ragweed, and another of white-tailed deer. A stream ecosystem could support populations of crayfish, snails, and the larval forms of mayflies.

Even though different ecosystems show a tremendous amount of variation, they are all alike in two important ways. Every ecosystem depends on a flow of

◄Mount Shuksan in Washington state is part of a forest ecosystem.

energy that begins with the sun. And within all ecosystems, nutrients are recycled.

Plants have the important job of capturing the sun's energy in a process called photosynthesis. The green material in plants—chlorophyll—makes photosynthesis possible. Within chlorophyll, carbon dioxide (a gas in the air) combines with water to make sugar and oxygen gas. Sugar and oxygen support many living things. Everything, even the green plants themselves, must have sugar to live. Plants, as well as almost all other living things, depend on oxygen, too. They use it during respiration, a process that converts food to a more useable type of energy.

Energy travels through the ecosystem along a path called a food chain. Because plants can capture the sun's energy, the food chain begins with plants, the producers. Animals get energy by eating plants or by eating plant-eating animals, so they are called consumers. When plants and animals die, decomposers go to work. Decomposers are organisms that include some fungi and microorganisms. Decomposers break down complex materials into simpler ones, getting energy for themselves and releasing nutrients back into the soil.

The living things in every ecosystem are specially adapted for life there. An adaptation is a feature that helps a living thing survive. Some adaptations are structural because they have to do with the organism's physical traits. For instance, some desert plants have a coating of wax on their leaves that prevents water loss. Other adaptations are behavioral. The migration of animals to warmer climates in the winter is a behavioral adaptation that helps them survive when temperatures are very low.

Over time, ecosystems go through natural changes. As physical factors such as light, oxygen, temperature, or rainfall vary, the populations in the ecosystems also change. When a landform, such as the lava flow from the eruption of a volcano, first appears, it is a barren place. The earliest inhabitants are usually lichens, small patches made up of fungi and simple plants. Lichens help break down the rock, speeding the process of soil formation. Eventually, plants settle in, adding their roots to the already crumbling lava rock. When the plants die and decompose, they contribute nutrients to the newly forming soil. These changes help other types of plants get a foothold, and eventually a flourishing ecosystem develops.

As an ecosystem matures, new groups of plants and animals move in. Each newcomer changes the system slightly. Over a long period of time, an ecosystem can be transformed from one type to another. For example, a pond ecosystem may gradually fill with sediment, eventually becoming a field. This process is called succession.

Ecologists study the features and relationships within ecosystems. They ask questions about how one kind of living thing influences another, or how a nonliving factor affects living things. By asking questions and conducting experiments, ecologists are learning to care for and preserve ecosystems.

EXPERIMENT 1.1

Living on the Edge

Question:

How do the life-forms in two neighboring ecosystems compare to those in the area where the two ecosystems meet?

Hypothesis:

A mixture of life-forms from both ecosystems will be observed where the two ecosystems meet.

Materials:

- **an adult**
- hula hoop (or a homemade hoop made of wire or some other bendable material)
- 2 bordering ecosystems
- meterstick or yardstick
- hand shovel
- science notebook and pencil
- field guides (optional)
- magnifying glass (optional)

In this experiment, you will sample the plant and animal populations in three locations: two bordering ecosystems and their mutual ecotone (see Figure 1a), the area where the two ecosystems overlap.

Procedure:

1. Find two neighboring ecosystems, plus their ecotone, that you want to study. For example, a forest and a nearby field are two ecosystems that share an ecotone with traits of both. A pond ecosystem and a scrub-land ecosystem are joined by a marshy area. If you live near a desert, the area between the desert and the semidry region nearby forms an ecotone. **Always go with an adult.**

2. With your science notebook, pencil, hula hoop, hand shovel, and a magnifying glass, if you have one, walk at least 9 meters (10 yards) into one of the ecosystems. Measure the distance with a meterstick or yard-stick. This will be called Ecosystem 1. Toss the hula hoop on the ground. Your first toss represents Trial 1 within Ecosystem 1.

Figure 1a.

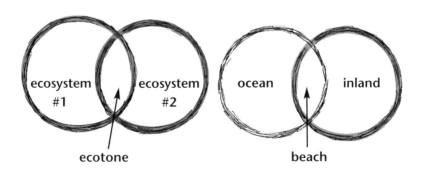

ecosystem #1   ecosystem #2   ocean   inland

ecotone   beach

An ecotone is formed in the area where two ecosystems overlap.

Figure 1b.

hula hoop

Count the number of plants you see inside the marked off area.

3. Carefully look at the area inside the hula hoop and count the number of different kinds of plants, or evidence of different kinds of plants, such as leaves, twigs, bark, and berries. (See Figure 1b.) If the leaves or stems of any trees or shrubs are hanging over the hula hoop, count them too. In your science notebook, make a tally mark for each different plant type you find within the area of the hula hoop. Record the total number of tally marks in your science notebook.

4. Now look in the hula hoop for animal life or evidence of animal life (a spiderweb, an anthill, or a chewed acorn). If you have a magnifying glass, use it to get a better look at the tiny animals. Do not just inspect the top of the soil. Dig underneath fallen leaves or a few inches into the soil. In your notebook, make one tally mark for each kind of animal you see, as well as a mark for each kind of animal evidence. Count the tally marks and record the total in your notebook.

5. Pick up your hula hoop and toss it somewhere else within this same ecosystem. This will be Trial 2 within Ecosystem 1. Once again count the number of different plant and animal species and record the totals. Repeat the process a third time for Trial 3 in Ecosystem 1. Record your data.

6. Calculate the average number of different types of plant and animal life for all three trials and record these numbers in your science notebook.

7. Take your science notebook, pencil, hula hoop, shovel, and magnifying glass at least 9 meters (10 yards) deep into the second ecosystem. This will be Ecosystem 2. Repeat the process of tossing the hula hoop for three different trials. Record your results for Ecosystem 2. Calculate the average once you complete three trials.

8. For the last sampling, take the hula hoop into the zone where these two ecosystems merge. Repeat the tossing technique in this area. Record your findings in your science notebook. Then calculate your average and record it. Which of the three areas showed the largest number of plant species? Animal species? How does biodiversity within an ecotone compare to biodiversity in the surrounding ecosystems?

Results and Conclusions

Ecosystems do not have clear, well-defined edges. You may even find it difficult to say exactly where a forest ecosystem starts and where it stops. That is because the edges of neighboring ecosystems merge into one another. The area where two ecosystems overlap is called an ecotone. Ecotones provide homes for living things from both ecosystems.

In this experiment, you saw how the biodiversity, the variety of living things, in two ecosystems affects what lives in the ecotone between them.

Science Project Ideas

- Extend your experiment by describing the characteristics of the plant and animal life in the two ecosystems and their ecotone. How are the plants and animals located in the ecotone alike? How are they different?

- Design and perform an experiment to compare the nonliving factors between the two ecosystems and their ecotone. Some factors that could be used for comparison include air temperature, soil temperature, light intensity, amount of water, and amount of wind exposure.

- If you hypothesize that ecotones are more diverse than the ecosystems they border, describe why it would be wise to sample a variety of different ecosystems and ecotones in your experiment. Do you think the size of the ecosystems and their ecotone would impact your hypothesis?

EXPERIMENT 1.2

The Climate Suits Me

Question:

What type of shelter best protects an animal from extreme cold?

Hypothesis:

Well-insulated shelters protect animals from cold.

Materials:

- **an adult**
- four 12-oz empty plastic bottles
- 4 alcohol-based out–door thermometers
- modeling clay
- 4 identical drinking glasses (large enough to hold the 12-oz bottles)
- funnel
- wood chips
- leaves and pine needles
- sand
- science notebook and pencil
- clock or watch
- masking tape
- marker
- small pitcher
- very hot tap water

Procedure:

1. Because you will be using hot water, have all of your materials ready and be prepared to work quickly—before the water gets cool. First, create four model animal shelters from four identical drinking glasses. Each glass must be large enough to hold a 12-oz bottle, with a few millimeters of space left between the bottle and the glass. Use masking tape and a marker to label one glass as OPEN AIR, one as SAND BURROW, one as WOOD CHIPS, and the last as LEAVES AND PINE NEEDLES.

2. To evaluate the four kinds of shelters, you must have four model animals. First, remove the labels from four empty 12-oz plastic bottles. **With the help of an adult**, fill a small pitcher with very hot water from the faucet. Insert a thermometer into the pitcher and hold it for one minute. Record the water's temperature in your science notebook as "Starting body temperature" for each of the four animals. Use a funnel to fill the four bottles so they are each three-quarters full of hot water. Make sure you have equal amounts of water in each bottle.

3. Place an outdoor, alcohol-based thermometer in each bottle. Put modeling clay around the mouth of each bottle to hold the thermometer in place and to seal the opening of the bottle.

4. Place one "animal," or bottle, in each of the four glasses. Add nothing more to the glass labeled OPEN AIR. The bottle in this glass represents an animal of the tundra living in the open. Pour sand into the glass labeled SAND BURROW until it comes up to the neck of the bottle. Stuff wood chips evenly into the glass labeled WOOD CHIPS until they come up to the neck of the bottle. Finally, stuff leaves and pine needles evenly into the glass labeled LEAVES AND PINE NEEDLES until they reach the neck of the bottle. (See Figure 2.)

5. Over the next eighteen minutes, read the temperature of the "animals" in each shelter every three minutes. Record all temperatures in your science notebook.

Figure 2.

Place each "animal" in its shelter. Which shelter best prevents heat loss?

6. Repeat the experiment, but this time place the protective material into each glass in this order: Wood chips, leaves and pine needles, open air, sand burrow. Record the results in your science notebook for trial 2. Compare the results of each trial. Based on your findings, what kind of shelter might provide the best protection from harsh tundra winters?

Results and Conclusions

The tundra is a vast, cold area near the North Pole that is home to fewer types of organisms than any other region of the earth. During the winter, animals living in the tundra must face extremely dry, cold conditions. To survive in such a challenging place, animals of the tundra are equipped with some unique adaptations.

In this experiment, you evaluated a behavioral adaptation, finding shelter, which helps some animals stay warm. Which shelter was most effective in preventing the loss of body heat from each "animal"? Which was least effective? Based on the results of this experiment, what kind of shelter would you build for yourself if you were stranded in the tundra?

 Science Project Ideas

- Design an experiment to test how body coverings, such as thick hair, feathers, or blubber, work to keep animals warm in the open air of a tundra winter.

- Conduct an experiment to show the effectiveness of some of the adaptations of animals that live in the desert.

- Dampen two sponges of the same size and mass. Find their masses by weighing them on a postage stamp scale. One sponge will be your control and the other will represent a desert plant. Devise different ways to help this "plant" retain as much water as possible over the next 48 hours. Both sponges must be kept in the same location, but you can add additional items to the one that represents a desert plant. What are some of your ideas for helping this "plant" conserve water? How do desert plants conserve water?

EXPERIMENT 1.3

In the Dark

Question:

How important is sunlight to an ecosystem?

Hypothesis:

Sunlight is essential for many living things in an ecosystem to survive.

Materials:

- **an adult**
- 2 widemouthed, glass gallon jars with lids
- ruler
- modeling clay
- gravel or sand
- aquarium charcoal
- 10 or 12 small plants (ferns, mosses, wildflowers); 2 of each type
- window with indirect sunlight
- wooded area
- 2 decaying pieces of wood
- small pebbles
- hand shovel
- garden gloves
- several insect collecting containers (empty margarine tubs with holes punched in their lids work well)

continued

continued

- water
- box (large enough to cover one of the jars)
- science notebook and pencil
- marker
- masking tape
- 2 pails
- paper cup
- sheets of newspaper

Procedure:

1. Go outdoors **with an adult** to a wooded area. Take two pails, a shovel, several insect collecting containers, and a pair of garden gloves to protect your hands.

2. In one pail, collect some dark, fertile soil. In the other, put ten or twelve small green plants, such as ferns and moss. Make sure you have two of each kind. Use the hand shovel to get as much of the roots and soil from around the roots as possible.

3. Check out the area for small animals, such as crickets, worms, or beetles. Any worms you collect should be placed in an insect collecting container along with the soil in which they are found. Place the crickets and beetles in a separate container without soil. Pick up a few small pebbles and two pieces of decaying wood and add them to your pail of soil.

4. Return indoors and set your collecting pails and containers aside while you prepare two mini-ecosystem jars. Spread newspapers on the floor and place the glass jars, lying on their sides, on top of them. To prevent the jars from rolling, wedge some modeling clay underneath each jar. (See Figure 3.)

Figure 3.

You can make two mini ecosystems. Place soil, gravel, and aquarium charcoal in each jar.

5. In the bottom of each jar, spread a one-centimeter (½-in) layer of aquarium charcoal. Top that with a one-centimeter (½-in) layer of gravel or sand. On top of this layer, place 7.5 centimeters (3 in) of soil that you collected in the forest. Use a paper cup to add enough water to the soil in both jars to moisten it thoroughly without creating any puddles.

6. With tape and a marker, label one jar as JAR A and the other as JAR B. Plant an equal number of the same types of plants in each jar. Add a piece of decaying wood and a couple of pebbles to each jar. Finally add the same kinds and number of animals to each jar. Put the lids on both jars.

7. In your science notebook, record the types and number of plants and animals you placed in each jar. Describe the starting condition of the plants: Include their color, whether they are wilting or firm, and the number of healthy and dead leaves on each. Record the starting conditions of the animals, including their activity levels.

8. To finish the first stage of your experiment, place a cardboard box over JAR B so that it does not receive any sunlight. The box must remain over JAR B at all times except for a few minutes when you observe the condition of life in the jar. Put JAR A near a window where it can receive indirect sunlight.

9. Every other day for the next 15 days, observe the condition of plant and animal life in each jar. Record your observations in your science notebook. If there is no change, write "No change." Record whether any plants have wilted, turned yellow, or died. Indicate whether the animals appear to be as active as they were when you captured them, or slower than they were. Make a note if any die. Look for the presence of molds— organisms that often prefer the dark. Describe any you see in your science notebook. At the end of Day 15, remove the living things from the jars and return them to where you captured them.

In a forest ecosystem, sunlight is essential for the success of plant life.

Results and Conclusions

All ecosystems take in energy to support living things. Most get this essential energy from the sun. The amount of light a system receives greatly influences the organisms that live there.

In your experiment, you deprived an ecosystem of sunlight for 15 days. In which jar did the plants stay the greenest? In which jar did the plants remain upright and unwilted? In which jar did more plants retain their leaves? In which jar were the animals the most active? In which jar did molds grow? From this experiment, can you make a statement describing some of the effects of sunlight on an ecosystem?

Science Project Ideas

- How could you repeat this experiment on an aquatic rather than a terrestrial ecosystem? What kind of results would you expect to get?

- Design an experiment that evaluates the impact of other key elements of an ecosystem, such as water.

- Create another homemade ecosystem, but instead of using woodland plants, use plants and animals from a grassland, a desert, or another type of ecosystem.

EXPERIMENT 1.4

My Plot or Yours?

Question:
Does plant diversity affect animal diversity in an ecosystem?

Hypothesis:
In an ecosystem, plant and animal diversity are related.

Materials:
- **an adult**
- string
- meterstick or yardstick
- 4 small wooden stakes
- hammer
- shovel
- garden gloves
- newspaper
- tweezers
- jar with holes punched in lid
- a piece of wire screen about the size of a dinner plate, or a large sieve with medium-sized openings
- science notebook and pencil
- sunny field or yard
- forest, shrubby area, or desert

In this experiment, you will find out if there is a relationship between plant species diversity and animal species diversity in your local ecosystems. To do so, you will sample the plant and animal populations in two different locations.

Procedure:

1. Go outdoors **with an adult** and locate a sunny field or a yard. Rope off a square of soil that has an area of one square meter (or one square yard). To do so, place the meterstick or yardstick flat on the ground. Hammer a wooden stake into the ground at each end of the stick, creating the first side of the square. Continue until all four stakes make a square. (See Figure 4a.) Tie a piece of a string around the stakes to rope off the square. This is Sample Plot 1.

2. Wearing garden gloves to protect your hands, examine the plants that are growing within Sample Plot 1. Count how many kinds of plants there are. Each kind, or species, of plant has unique characteristics. One species may have slender leaves, while another may have fan-shaped leaves. Notice that some of the small and large plants may be of the same species, but different sizes and ages. In your science notebook, write the number of plant species you found growing in Sample Plot 1.

3. Look for animals, such as ants or centipedes, in the area. Note the number of animal species you see. For example, three black ants

Figure 4a.

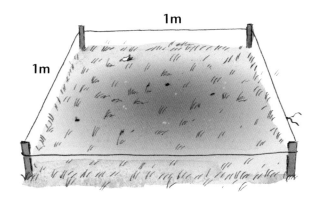

Hammer stakes in the ground one meter apart.
The square you make will be Sample Plot 1.

represent one species, and two crickets represent another species. Record the number of kinds of animals in your science notebook.

4. Look more closely at the surface of the soil in Sample Plot 1 for evidence of animal life. You may see scat (animal feces), tracks, holes in the ground, or the remnants of food, such as nutshells. Record the kinds of animal evidence you see.

5. Spread a piece of newspaper on the ground. Dig up three or four shovelfuls of soil and place them on the newspaper. Remove any sticks, rocks, or leaves from the soil.

Figure 4b.

Using a screen or a sieve, sift the soil to look for animals.

6. Place a piece of screen or a sieve on another piece of newspaper. Shovel some of the soil you collected onto the screen. Lift the screen gently and shake it back and forth, sifting the soil onto the newspaper. (See Figure 4b.) Watch for small animals that drop through or get caught in the screen. Gently collect them with tweezers and place them in a jar.

7. Repeat the sifting procedure until all of the soil has been examined. Record the total number of animal species and animal evidence. This represents the number of animal species in Sample Plot 1. When you have recorded all of your data, return the animals to the soil.

8. Select a different type of ecosystem, such as a forest, a desert, or a shrubby area. Create Sample Plot 2 and repeat the entire procedure. Record your results. In which sample plot did you find the most species of plants? In which did you find the most species of animals?

Results and Conclusions

Every species in an ecosystem plays an essential role. The loss of even one species can change the entire system. Individual species in an ecosystem can be compared to bricks in a building. The removal of one brick may seem to make very little difference. But as more and more bricks are lost, the building becomes weaker. Eventually, it collapses entirely. In the same way, any factor that reduces an ecosystem's biodiversity, or variety of organisms, may damage it.

Every ecosystem is unique, with it own particular collection of living things and physical factors. Some, such as marshy areas along coastlines, have very few plant species, but many animal species. Others, such as tropical rain forests, have a wide variety of plants and animals. Ecologists must study each type of ecosystem to understand the interactions in it.

How useful was your experiment in determining the number of different plant and animal species living in a given area? From this experiment, could you make a statement relating the number of plant species growing in an area to the number of animal species living there? Why or why not?

Science Project Ideas

- To get the best results, repeat your sampling technique in several areas. Select a plot in a third ecosystem to improve your experimental data. In what other types of ecosystems could you rope off sample plots?

- Other life-forms in an ecosystem include fungi and microscopic organisms. How could you include these living things in your research on biodiversity?

- Design and perform an experiment to compare biodiversity in an area that is heavily populated by people to an area that is not heavily populated by people.

EXPERIMENT 1.5

Soil Survivors

Question:

How does animal life in the soil of a field compare to animal life in forest soil?

Hypothesis:

By examining samples of soil from a field and a forest, the animal life can be compared.

Materials:

- **an adult**
- 2 empty 2-liter soda bottles (clean, with the labels removed)
- scissors
- hand shovel
- 2 desk lamps with 100-watt bulbs
- two 10-centimeter by 10-centimeter (4-in by 4-in) pieces of wire screen
- masking tape
- garden gloves
- ruler
- tweezers

continued

continued

- 2 large, resealable plastic bags
- magnifying glass
- pictures of soil invertebrates from a reference book (optional)
- newspaper
- marker
- jar with holes punched in the lid
- science notebook and pencil
- table
- moist, leaf-littered area in open field
- forest

Procedure:

1. Start by setting up two insect collection devices. To make one, cut an empty 2-liter soda bottle in half. The bottle cap is not needed. Place the bottom half of the bottle on a table. (The table should be near an electrical outlet because you will be using a lamp.) Fit a piece of wire screen inside the mouth of the bottle. (See Figure 5.) Put the top half of the bottle upside down into the bottom half of the bottle. Securely tape the two bottle halves together. You have made a Berlese funnel. Now create a second Berlese funnel just like the first one.

Figure 5.

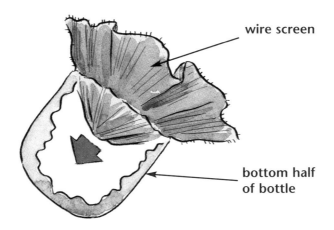

wire screen

bottom half
of bottle

Line the mouth of the bottle with screen.

2. **With an adult**, go outdoors and locate a moist, leaf littered area in an open field. (Moist areas are homes to more animal life than dry ones.) Wearing garden gloves to protect your hands and using a hand shovel, fill one plastic bag with a combination of leaf litter, decaying material under the leaf litter, and the top 5 centimeters (2 in) of soil. Label this bag as FIELD. Go to a forest and repeat this process, placing the collected material in the second bag, which you should label as FOREST.

3. Take the two samples indoors. Empty the contents of the FIELD bag onto a piece of newspaper. Wearing gloves, sift through the sample and look for evidence of animal life. If you have a magnifying glass, use it to get a closer look. When you find an organism, pick it up very gently with your tweezers and place it in a jar. Cover the jar so the organism does not escape. (Make sure there are holes in the lid so that the organism will have enough air.) Once you have collected all the organisms you can see, examine them closely. Categorize each into one of the following groups, using a reference book if you have one, to identify the different organisms:

a. Insects (with 6 legs, such as beetles and ladybugs)

b. Arachnids (with 8 legs, such as spiders, scorpions, mites, and ticks)

c. Worms (no legs)

d. Snails and slugs (snails have shells and slugs do not; both leave a trail of slime)

e. Many legs (such as millipedes, centipedes, and pill bugs)

f. Larvae or undeveloped invertebrates (short, worm-like organisms; some may have legs on one end of their bodies)

4. Place a tally mark in your science notebook beside the appropriate classification group each time you find a new animal. When you have looked at the entire sample, add the tally marks together and record the total. Then release the organisms outside.

5. Place the litter, decaying material, and topsoil from the field sample into the top of one of the Berlese funnels. Toss any unused portion of the field

sample outdoors. Write the word FIELD on an index card and place the card in front of the funnel. Position a lamp 10 centimeters (4 in) directly above the sample. (See Figure 6.) Turn on the lamp.

Figure 6.

Place a lamp over each Berlese funnel.

6. Repeat the above process with the sample from the forest and the second Berlese funnel. Once you have placed the sample from the forest in the second funnel and turned on the light, put an index card with the word FOREST in front of the setup.

7. Leave the two funnels set up for the next 48 hours. At the end of this time, turn off the lights. You should find organisms walking, crawling, and flying inside the bottom half of each bottle. Classify these organisms as you did before. Record your results in your science notebook. Take the Berlese funnels outdoors, remove the tape, and release the organisms. Dump the soil and leaf litter outdoors.

The plants of an ecosystem make up its flora, and the animals, such as deer, make up its fauna.

Results and Conclusions

The surface of a field or a forest may look like a lifeless carpet of leaves, grass, and dirt. But if you take a close look at either, you can find a busy community of animals. All of the animals in an ecosystem make up the fauna. Topsoil and the material on it, the litter, contain the richest faunas you can find. Most of the animals found there are invertebrates, animals without backbones.

In this experiment, you compared the faunas of the litter and topsoil ecosystems in a field and a forest. These ecosystems differ in many respects, and two of their most important differences are temperature and amounts of moisture. These factors have a major impact on the fauna.

In which of the two ecosystems (forest or field) did you find more variety of organisms? Why do you think so? Which of the two ecosystems had the greatest total number of soil organisms? What classification group was the dominant one in the field? In the forest?

 # Science Project Ideas

- Determine if there is a difference in the number and types of invertebrates found in the litter from those found in the topsoil. Design an experiment to see which contains more organisms.

- Design an experiment to see if the population of invertebrates in a litter and soil ecosystem changes from season to season.

- Do you think the amount of moisture would affect an animal's life in the soil? Would the temperature affect it? The shade? Conduct an experiment to find these answers.

CHAPTER 2

Nonliving Factors Affect Ecosystems

An ecosystem is made up of living and nonliving components. Some of the nonliving factors are temperature, moisture, minerals, wind, and light. Three of these factors—temperature, moisture, and wind—are largely determined by the climate of an area. Think about the differences in the climates of Alaska and Florida.

Moisture may be one of the most critical factors to the survival of the living components of the system. Without water, life as we know it would not exist on this planet. Even though Earth has a lot of water, the planet will never get any more, so what is here is constantly recycled and reused. Moisture drops to the earth from the sky in the form or rain, snow, sleet, or fog. Some water is taken in by living things. Some of it soaks into the ground and makes its way to deep reservoirs. Most of the water runs off soil and into streams, rivers, and

◄ This corn seedling is affected by such nonliving factors as temperature, moisture, light, and wind.

oceans. Water goes back into the atmosphere by evaporation from living things and nonliving surfaces. This cycle has been going on for billions of years.

Like water, the nutrients in an ecosystem are constantly being recycled. Soil contains various levels of essential minerals, such as nitrogen, phosphorus, and sulfur. Carbon dioxide and oxygen, two life-supporting gases, are found in air, soil, and living things. All of the nutrients are taken into living things, then returned to the environment for reuse.

Soil characteristics, such as the sizes and shapes of soil particles, have an impact on the organisms that live in it. Small, closely packed soil particles reduce the amount of water and oxygen in soil. Those particles are favored by living things that prefer damp, poorly oxygenated environments. On the other hand, large, loosely combined soil particles create good homes for organisms that must have high levels of oxygen and drier environments.

Light is the source of life in most ecosystems because it supplies energy. Without light, plants could not make food, and there would be no energy to support living things. Unlike water and nutrients, which are recycled, light energy travels through an ecosystem on a one-way path, from its producer—the sun—to consumers and decomposers. Along this path, some energy is lost as heat.

Ecologists study the impact that various physical factors have on living things. By doing so, they can better understand how ecosystems work.

EXPERIMENT 2.1

Thirsty Little Sprouts

Question:

Do seeds require moisture to germinate?

Hypothesis:

Seeds need water to germinate.

Materials:

- package of radish seeds
- science notebook and pencil
- 2 jar lids that are the same size
- sponge
- 2 shoeboxes
- water
- magnifying glass
- scissors

Procedure:

1. Use scissors to cut a sponge into two pieces of equal size. Each piece should be small enough to fit in one of the jar lids.

2. Dip one sponge in lukewarm water, then squeeze out the excess. Place this sponge in a jar lid. Add enough water to cover the bottom of the lid. Place the dry sponge in the other jar lid. Spread 10 radish seeds evenly over the wet sponge and 10 more seeds on the dry sponge.

Figure 7.

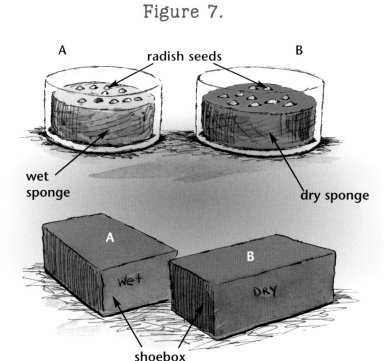

A   radish seeds   B

wet
sponge   dry sponge

A   wet

B   DRY

shoebox

Place the seeds on top of the sponges inside the jar lids.

3. Cover each lid with a shoebox. Write the letter A on the box placed over
   the wet sponge and the letter B on the box over the dry sponge. (See
   Figure 7.) The boxes help keep the seeds in the dark, just as if the seeds
   were buried in the soil.

4. Each day for the next ten days, lift the box from each sponge and count
   the total number of radish seeds that have germinated. Radish seeds
   that germinate will have fuzzy white threads sticking out of the seed.

You may need to use a magnifying glass to see them. Before putting the lid back over the sponges, make sure that SPONGE A is still wet. If it feels dry, add water to the jar lid.

At the end of ten days you may dispose of the radish seeds or save them for one of the science project ideas that follow this experiment.

5. On Day 10, calculate the percentage of seeds that germinated on SPONGE A. To do this, divide the total number of seeds that germinated by 10, then multiply by 100. Record this number in your science notebook. Repeat this calculation for SPONGE B. On which sponge—wet or dry—was there the most germination?

Results and Conclusions

Many plants produce seeds. Inside each seed is a plant embryo, complete with its own small leaves, stems, and roots. A seed produces enough food to support a growing embryo for the first several days of its life. The growth of a young plant from its seed is called germination.

There are several physical factors in the environment that control when germination begins. A tiny plant will remain trapped in its seed until the conditions are just right. This is nature's way of making sure that seeds don't germinate when it is too cold or dry for the plant to grow.

Based on the findings of this experiment, do you think moisture is an important factor in germination of radish seeds? What might happen with a different kind of seed?

Science Project Ideas

- What other factors do you think affect seed germination? Test one or more of these factors in your own experiment.

- Can seeds get too much water? Design an experiment to find out.

- Divide the radish seeds that germinated into two groups. Plant each group in soil in a Styrofoam cup. Water one of the cups of seeds daily, but allow the other cup to remain dry. Decide if moisture is necessary for radish plant growth after germination.

- Try this experiment with other kinds of seeds.

- Devise an experiment to determine whether exposure to light affects the rate at which some seeds germinate.

EXPERIMENT 2.2

A Drop in the Bag

Question:

How does the amount of sunlight affect water loss from a plant?

Hypothesis:

Intense sunlight increases water loss in plants.

Materials:

- **an adult**
- 3 large, clear garbage bags
- 2 large measuring cups
- 3 long pieces of string
- 3 fist-sized rocks
- pencil with a sharp point
- science notebook and pencil
- calculator
- 1 tree or shrub in a sunny area
- 1 tree or shrub of the same type in a shaded area
- 1 tree or shrub of the same type in a partially shaded area

Procedure:

1. When the weather forecast is for sun for the next 24 hours, select a type of tree or shrub that is common in your area. For this experiment, it is best to choose a type with low limbs and leaves instead of needles. Find that type of tree or shrub in an area that receives sun all day and call it TREE 1. Choose a leafy branch that you can reach. Count the number of leaves on the branch. Record this number in your science notebook.

2. Drop a fist-sized rock in a large, clear garbage bag; it will serve as a weight that helps water collect in the bottom of the bag. Slide the bag onto the branch so that you cover all of the leaves you just counted. Arrange the rock in the bag so that it is hanging below the branch. (See Figure 8a.) Gather the open end of the bag around the branch and secure it with a string.

3. Find a tree of the same species and similar size that is located in an ecosystem of complete shade, one where no direct light penetrates. This is TREE 2. Repeat the entire procedure used for TREE 1, recording the number of leaves in your science notebook.

4. Locate a third tree of the same size and type that is located in a partially shaded ecosystem, one that receives some light, but not full sunlight. Call this TREE 3. Repeat the procedure used for the previous two trees, recording the number of leaves in your science notebook.

5. Twenty-four hours later, **ask an adult** to help you when you return to TREE 1. Carry two measuring cups, a sharp pencil, and your science notebook. Hold a measuring cup beneath the water that has collected in the plastic bag. Have a second cup nearby in case there is more than one cupful of water. With a sharp pencil, punch a hole in the bag so the water runs into the cup. Record the amount of water you collect. Pour out the water and remove the bag and string from the tree.

Figure 8a.

rock

Slide a clear garbage bag over a limb and secure it with a string.

6. Repeat the water-measuring process on TREE 2 and TREE 3. Record your results.

7. To calculate the amount of water produced by each leaf on TREE 1, divide the amount of water collected by the number of leaves. Repeat the calculations for TREE 2 and TREE 3, entering your data into your science notebook.

Results and Conclusions

Trees and other plants absorb water primarily through their roots. Water travels from roots to leaves through a system of very small tubes. During the day, much of this water evaporates from tiny holes in a plant's leaves. This process of water loss is called transpiration. In most plants, 90 percent of water absorbed by the roots is lost through transpiration.

Each tiny opening in a leaf is called a stoma (plural is stomata). The size of the opening is controlled by a pair of guard cells. When guard cells take in water they swell outward, causing the stoma to enlarge. When the guard cells lose water they shrink and the stoma decreases in size. (See Figure 8b.)

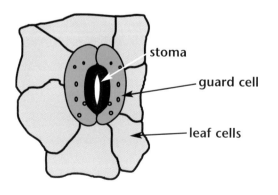

stoma

guard cell

leaf cells

Figure 8b.

Guard cells surround each stoma in a leaf.

The size of the stomata on leaves determines the rate of transpiration. Fully open stomata allow for maximum transpiration. Closed stomata halt transpiration.

In this experiment, you compared the rate of transpiration of plants of the same species found in different ecosystems. What factor in your experiment do you think affected the amount of water transpired by the leaves on each tree?

 Science Project Ideas

- What other factors could influence the amount of water a tree transpires? Do you think that windy conditions would increase or decrease transpiration? How about the amount of humidity in the air? Design an experiment to compare transpiration in two trees exposed to different amounts of wind.

- If you wanted to determine how much water an entire tree transpired in twenty-four hours, how could you do so?

- How could you design an experiment to compare transpiration in one tree or shrub during different seasons?

- How could you design an experiment to compare how transpiration varies between different species of trees?

EXPERIMENT 2.3

Fermentation Factories

Question:

Is temperature a factor in yeast fermentation?

Hypothesis:

Temperature can affect the rate of yeast fermentation.

Materials:

- **an adult**
- string
- package of baker's yeast
- science notebook and pencil
- 4 Styrofoam cups large enough to hold 130 milliliters (4 oz) of water
- clock or watch
- 4 rubber bands
- water
- measuring cup

- 4 empty 12-ounce plastic bottles
- 4 alcohol-based thermometers
- 4 round balloons
- ruler
- ice
- microwave oven
- sugar
- tablespoon
- microwave-safe container
- marker

Procedure:

1. Label four empty bottles as A, B, C, and D. Place one tablespoon of sugar and one tablespoon of active dry yeast in each bottle. Set these aside while you prepare four water solutions.

2. Label four Styrofoam cups as A, B, C, and D. Use a measuring cup to put 130 milliliters (4 oz) of cool water into CUP A. Drop in one small ice cube, then set this cup aside.

3. Next, adjust the temperature of the water coming out of your tap until an alcohol-based thermometer held in the water reads 21°C (70°F). In a measuring cup, collect 130 milliliters (4 oz) of 21°C-water and pour it into CUP B.

4. Next, adjust the temperature of the water coming out of your tap to 38°C (100°F). Collect 130 milliliters (4 oz) of 38°C water in the measuring cup, and then pour it into CUP C. For the water in CUP D, collect 130 milliliters in a measuring cup. Pour the water into a microwave-safe container and put it in a microwave oven. Heat the water for 30 seconds. **Ask an adult** to remove the water from the microwave and use a thermometer to see if the temperature has reached 66°C (150°F). **Do not place the thermometer in the microwave.** Pour the water into CUP D.

5. Record the temperatures of the water in all four cups in your science notebook. Pour the water from CUP A into BOTTLE A. Pick up BOTTLE A and swirl to mix the water with the sugar and the yeast. Quickly stretch the open end of a balloon over the mouth of the bottle. Wrap a rubber band around the mouth of the balloon where it covers the bottle opening. Pour the contents of CUP B into BOTTLE B, swirl, and

Figure 9.

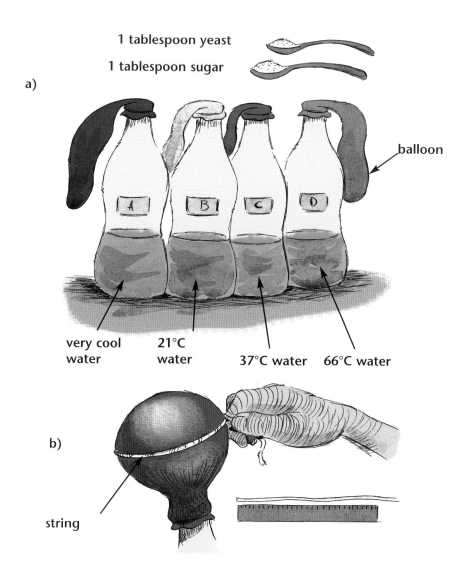

a) Add yeast and sugar to bottles of water at different temperatures.
b) Measure the circumference of each balloon.

cover with a balloon. Repeat this process for BOTTLE C and BOTTLE D. (See Figure 9a.) Yeasts that undergo fermentation produce carbon dioxide gas, which will cause the balloons to inflate. The bigger the balloon gets, the greater the rate of fermentation.

6. Every 5 minutes, for the next 30 minutes, measure the circumference of each balloon. (See Figure 9b.) To do this, wrap a string around the widest point of the balloon. Remove the string and use a ruler to measure the length of the string. In your science notebook, record each balloon's circumference in centimeters. If a balloon does not inflate, write zero in your notebook.

7. After 30 minutes, remove the balloons and dispose of the yeast mixtures. Which balloon got the biggest? Which balloon increased in size the fastest? Which balloon was the smallest?

Results and Conclusions

We are surrounded by fungi. Some of the most common types are yeasts, molds, mildews, and mushrooms. You may have seen fungi growing on the ground or on the side of a tree.

Fungi, like all living things, need food. They use food to make the energy that keeps them alive. Organisms change food into energy in one of two ways: by respiration or by fermentation. Plants, animals, and many fungi undergo respiration. In this process, their cells break down food in the presence of oxygen. As a result, they make a lot of energy and two by-products: carbon dioxide gas and water. Yeasts, however, use the process of fermentation. During fermentation, organisms change food into a smaller quantity of energy without oxygen. While doing so, they yield three by-products: alcohol, water, and carbon dioxide gas.

Even though there are more than 160 different species of yeast living all around you, you probably have not seen many. Yeasts are one-celled fungi, so they are hard to spot. Baker's yeast is used to make bread. When baker's yeast is combined with bread dough, the yeast cells become active and undergo fermentation. Carbon dioxide gas given off during fermentation is what causes the bread to rise.

Certain conditions must be met for yeast to undergo fermentation. Food and water must be present and the temperature must be warm. A change in food, temperature, or moisture affects the rate of fermentation and the rate at which yeasts grow.

In this experiment, you found out how a change in temperature alters the rate at which yeasts carry out fermentation. Based on your data, how does temperature affect the rate of fermentation in yeasts? In the soil, wild yeasts help break down dead plants and animals. From this experiment, do you think that wild yeasts are more active in the summer or winter? Would you expect dead plants and animals to decay faster in warm weather or in cold weather?

Bread mold is a fungus whose growth can be easily observed.

Science Project Ideas

- Conduct an experiment to find out how different foods (sources of sugar) affect the rate of fermentation.

- Bread mold is also a fungus. Conduct an experiment to find out the best temperature for bread mold growth. You can collect bread mold spores by leaving bread unwrapped for 24 hours. **Caution:** *Once you have started this experiment, keep the bread in a resealable plastic bag, because some people are allergic to mold spores. Do not open the bag; view the mold through the plastic.*

EXPERIMENT 2.4

Cool Fish

Question:

How do temperatures affect the breathing rate and activity of fish?

Hypothesis:

Cool temperatures will slow the respiration and activity of goldfish.

Materials:

- 3 goldfish of about equal size (sold at any pet store)
- aquarium
- goldfish food
- dip net
- ice
- thermometer
- 3 quart jars
- clear bowl that is large enough to easily hold a quart jar
- watch or clock with a second hand
- science notebook and pencil
- marker
- water

Procedure:

1. Prepare a fish bowl or aquarium by filling it with tap water two days before buying your fish. Also put water in three quart jars. Label these jars A, B, and C. During this time, the water will reach room temperature, and any chlorine in the water will evaporate. If you do not know how to maintain a fish bowl or aquarium, consult an expert at the pet store.

2. Purchase three goldfish of about the same size. Do not forget to buy some fish food. Following directions from the pet store, introduce the fish to your aquarium. **Remember: The fish is a living animal. Never expose it to water that is too hot or too cold**. Allow the fish 24 hours to get used to their new home before beginning the experiment.

3. The following day, shake up or stir the water in the three jars to make sure that it contains plenty of oxygen. Use a dip net to remove the three fish from the aquarium. Place one in JAR A, one in JAR B, and one in JAR C.

4. Take the temperature of the water in JAR A and record it in your science notebook. Closely observe the gill covers of the fish in this jar. (The gill covers are flaps of skin that protect the gills.) Watch them open and close as the fish pulls water over its gills to supply its body with oxygen. Count the number of times the gill flaps open in 15 seconds. Multiply this number by 4 to find the respiration rate of the fish for 60 seconds. Record that number in your science notebook for JAR A. Put the fish back in the aquarium and watch it move. For 60 seconds, count the number of turns or shifts in direction the fish makes as it swims. Record this number in your notebook for activity level. Remove the fish from the aquarium and place it back in JAR A.

5. Place JAR B in a clear bowl. (See Figure 10.) Put a few ice cubes and some tap water in the bowl. Insert a thermometer in JAR B. When the temperature has dropped 5 degrees below the temperature of the water in JAR A, observe the fish in JAR B and count the number of times the gill covers open in 15 seconds. Multiply this number by 4 and record it in your science notebook for respiration. Remove JAR B from the bowl. Place the fish in the aquarium and watch how many times the fish changes direction over the next minute. Record this information in your science notebook. Remove the fish from the aquarium and place it back in JAR B.

6. Place JAR C in the glass bowl filled with ice water. Allow the jar to remain there until the temperature in JAR C drops 10 degrees below the temperature of JAR A. Record this temperature in your science notebook. Repeat the same procedure you used with the first two fish and record your results.

7. After you have gathered your data, return all three fish to the aquarium. Give the fish a permanent home in a large aquarium at your house or school.

Results and Conclusions

In this experiment, you observed how goldfish are affected by temperature changes in their environment. Which of the fish had the slowest respiration? Which had the highest respiration? Which fish was the most active? Which was the least active?

Each kind of living thing survives best within a certain range of temperatures. The body temperature of humans and other warm-blooded

Figure 10.

Place JAR B in a bowl of ice water.

animals remains about the same, no matter what the temperatures are around them. This is not the case with cold-blooded animals, such as fish, amphibians, and reptiles. Their internal body temperatures change as the temperatures around them rise or fall. Temperature influences breathing rate and level of activity in cold-blooded animals. Therefore, it also affects their feeding habits and reproductive behaviors.

Goldfish are cold-blooded animals whose breathing rate and level of activity are affected by temperature.

 Science Project Ideas

- Repeat this procedure, giving each fish a trial in each experimental jar on three other occasions. Are your results consistent each time you do the experiment?

- Which do you think would be more active: goldfish living in the dark or goldfish living in moderate light? Why? Conduct an experiment to find out, taking care not to deprive any fish of light for more than one hour.

EXPERIMENT 2.5

The Right Light

Question:

How do differences in light intensity affect the behavior of earthworms?

Hypothesis:

Earthworms prefer environments without intense light.

Materials:

- **an adult**
- shoebox with lid
- 6 earthworms
- 3 flashlights
- wax paper
- plastic wrap
- black construction paper
- clear tape
- moist topsoil
- scissors
- watch or clock
- ruler
- marker
- nail or ice pick
- science notebook and pencil

Procedure:

1. Prepare an earthworm box. On one side of a shoebox, draw three evenly spaced squares that are 8 centimeters by 8 centimeters (about 3 in by 3 in). With scissors, cut along the lines you made to form three small windows in the box. Tape a square of clear plastic wrap over one opening. Tape a piece of wax paper over the middle opening. Tape a piece of black construction paper over the third window. **Ask an adult** to punch about 20 small air holes in the box top with a nail or an ice pick.

2. Sprinkle a 2.5-centimeter (1-in) layer of moist garden soil or topsoil in the bottom of the shoebox. Place three flashlights on a table about 5 centimeters (2 in) from each window so that light is shining in all three windows. Put all six earthworms in the box. Two should be placed directly behind each of the three windows. Place the cover on the box. (See Figure 11.)

3. Every 15 minutes for the next hour open the lid of the shoebox and locate the six worms. Make notes about the location of each worm in your science notebook. Release the worms in a wooded area.

Shine a light in each window of the experimental box.

Earthworms live in soil, often away from direct light.

Results and Conclusions

Earthworms live in the soil. There they dine on organic matter, such as decaying leaves, and they leave behind small piles of mineral-rich waste called castings. Earthworms prefer some environments to others.

In this experiment, you tested an earthworm's preference for light intensity. Did the worms prefer a certain location in the box? What was the significance of the different coverings over the windows in this experiment? Based on this data, how does light intensity affect earthworm behavior?

Science Project Ideas

- Devise an experiment to find out how earthworms respond to surfaces of different textures, such as rough cloth, silky cloth, paper, and sandpaper.

- Are earthworms the only animals that respond to differences in light intensity? Find some sowbugs (pillbugs) under damp pine needles or in garden soil. Conduct an experiment to test their reaction to light.

- Conduct an experiment to see how different amounts of moisture affect earthworms or sowbugs. Try using sponges holding varying amounts of water to test the preference of the animals to very wet, wet, damp, or dry conditions.

CHAPTER 3

Living Factors Affect Ecosystems

E ach organism in an ecosystem, whether it is a producer, consumer, or decomposer, lives alongside other organisms. Plants and animals of the same species may share or compete for resources, such as food or space. Plants also share or compete with each other for light and water.

Organisms of different species are constantly interacting, too. Deer graze on the young buds of woody plants, and mice eat the seeds of grasses. These and many other practices by animals affect the growth of plant populations. Many animals have predator and prey relationships. For example, a population of owls may be the predators of a population of mice, their

◄ Lichens, which grow on the bark of trees and rocks, are made of fungi and algae. The fungi and algae help each other survive.

prey. The size of the owl population determines the size of the mouse population. But the size of the mouse population regulates the size of the owl population as well. The owl population preys on the mice, limiting the mouse population. At the same time, the owl population cannot grow too large because there would not be enough mice to go around. To maintain long-term populations, predators and their prey must find a delicate balance.

Balance is also the key to survival for plants and the animals that eat them. If an animal population grows so large that it overgrazes and destroys the plants on which it feeds, then the animals are left without food. For example, if large populations of deer eat all of the young plants that provide their food, the plant population is damaged or eliminated from the ecosystem. As a result, the deer's food supply disappears.

Some organisms have very close relationships. Mutualism is a relationship in which two things live together to benefit both. Lichens, which look like small, crusty spots, are found on trees and rocks. They are actually made up of two types of organisms, fungi and green or blue-green algae. These two living things have a mutualistic relationship: Fungi provide the pair with shelter and moisture, and algae produce food for both.

In some cases, only one of the organisms in a close relationship is benefited, but the other is not harmed in any way. This type of relationship is called commensalism. The remora fish that ride along with sharks are commensals. When sharks feed, the remoras dine on any leftovers floating in the water. Yet their presence on sharks does not seem to impact the sharks in any way.

A relationship in which one member is harmed but the other benefits is called parasitism. A tick living on a dog is a parasite. Parasites can be found living on almost all species of plants and animals.

EXPERIMENT 3.1

Give Me Space

Question:

Do alfalfa seeds release chemicals that interfere with the germination of other seeds?

Hypothesis:

Alfalfa seeds can prevent other seeds from germinating.

Materials:

- 5 jar lids of the same size
- 50 radish seeds
- 50 alfalfa seeds
- paper towels
- scissors
- medicine dropper
- water
- science notebook and pencil
- plastic wrap
- marker

Procedure:

1. With scissors, trim a paper towel into a circle that will fit snugly into a jar lid. Use it as a pattern to cut four more paper towel circles and put them inside four other jar lids. Use a marker to label the outside of the jar lids as A, B, C, D, and E.

2. With a medicine dropper, drip water into LID A until the paper towel is completely damp. Drain any excess water from the lid. Repeat this process for LIDS B, C, D, and E.

3. Next, sprinkle 20 alfalfa seeds on top of the paper towel in LID A. Sprinkle 20 radish seeds on top of the paper towel in LID B. Sprinkle 10 alfalfa and 10 radish seeds into LID C. Sprinkle 15 alfalfa and 5 radish seeds in LID D. Sprinkle 15 radish and 5 alfalfa seeds into LID E.

4. Stretch a piece of plastic wrap over each lid so it fits tightly across the top. Use a sharp pencil to gently punch five small holes into all five plastic wrap coverings. (See Figure 12.)

5. Put the five jar lids in a dark place. Each day check the lids and record the total number of seeds of each type that have germinated. Continue the process for 10 days. Record your findings. How did the germination rates of combined radish and alfalfa seeds in LIDS C, D, and E compare to the germination rates of the individual seeds in LIDS A and B?

Save the alfalfa and radish seedlings for the science project ideas that follow.

Figure 12.

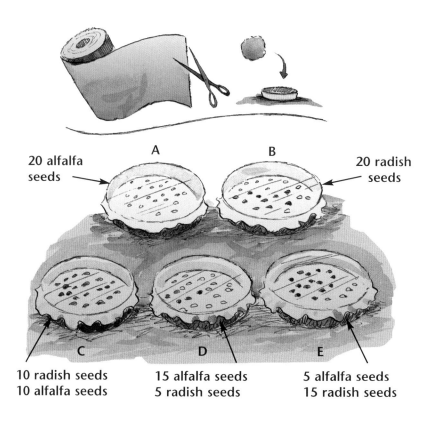

20 alfalfa
seeds

A

B

20 radish
seeds

C

10 radish seeds
10 alfalfa seeds

D

15 alfalfa seeds
5 radish seeds

E

5 alfalfa seeds
15 radish seeds

Use five jar lids, along with alfalfa seeds and radish
seeds, to find out if alfalfa seeds are allelopathic.

Results and Conclusions

Some plants release chemicals that prevent other plants from growing too near to them. Black walnut trees and some other plants are described as allelopathic because they have the ability to protect their space. Allelopathic plants release chemicals that keep other plants from growing close to them. Sunflowers, sweet potatoes, and sagebrushes are just a few other allelopathic plants known to use this space-protecting method.

Different plants release allelopathic chemicals in different ways. In some, leaves produce chemicals in the form of a gas. The gas travels from the leaves to the air surrounding the plant, creating a kind of invisible barrier. In other plants, chemicals enter the ground when leaves drop off and decay. Some plants put their allelopathic chemicals directly into the soil from their roots. Whatever their method, allelopathic plants use chemicals to keep other plant species at a distance.

In your experiment, did you observe allelopathy? Did germination rates decrease for radish seeds when alfalfa seeds were present? Did the quantity of alfalfa seeds seem to affect radish germination? Based on your results, do you think alfalfa or radish seeds exhibit allelopathy?

Science Project Ideas

- Plant some of the radish seedlings alone, some alfalfa seedlings alone, and some radish and alfalfa seedlings together. Measure their growth rate to see if the alfalfa slows radish growth.

- Try another allelopathy experiment but use the leaves of other types of plants known to be allelopathic. See if germination of radishes is slowed by the presence of yam, sunflower, or sage leaves.

- Devise an experiment to test how well plants germinate and grow in soil collected from under a black walnut tree.

EXPERIMENT 3.2

Pesky Plants!

Question:

When do weeds interfere with the growth of radish plants?

Hypothesis:

When weeds become invasive, they interfere with radish plants.

Materials:

- **an adult**
- 80 radish seeds
- 140 rye grass seeds
- 4 empty plastic cups of the same size (yogurt or margarine cups)
- water
- marker
- ruler
- ice pick or nail
- science notebook and pencil
- potting soil
- measuring cup
- pan that will hold all four plastic cups
- window with indirect sunlight

Procedure:

1. **Have an adult** use a nail or an ice pick to place 5 holes in the bottom of each of four plastic cups. Fill each cup with potting soil to within 2.5 centimeters (1 in) of the top. Use a marker to label the cups A, B, C, and D.

2. In this experiment, radishes represent cultivated plants and rye grass represents weeds. Sprinkle 20 radish seeds in CUP A. Cover the seeds completely with about one centimeter (about ½ in) of soil. In CUP B, sprinkle 20 radish seeds and 20 rye grass seeds. Cover the seeds with soil. In CUP C, spread 20 radish seeds and 40 rye grass seeds, then cover with soil. In CUP D, place 20 radish seeds and 80 rye grass seeds, then cover with soil. (See Figure 13.)

3. Place the four cups in a pan. Use a measuring cup to pour enough water into CUP A to moisten, but not soak, the soil. Add the same amount of water to the other three cups. Place the pan with the cups near a window that gets indirect sunlight.

4. Check the cups each day to make sure the soil is still damp. Add water as necessary, giving the same amount of water to all four. At the end of the first week, count how many radish and how many rye grass seeds have germinated in each cup. Place these totals into your notebook. Measure the height of each radish plant in CUP A. Add the heights, then divide by the total number of radish plants to get a height average. Record this average in your notebook. Do the same for the radish plants in the other three cups. You do not need to record information on the germination or height of the rye grass seeds.

Figure 13.

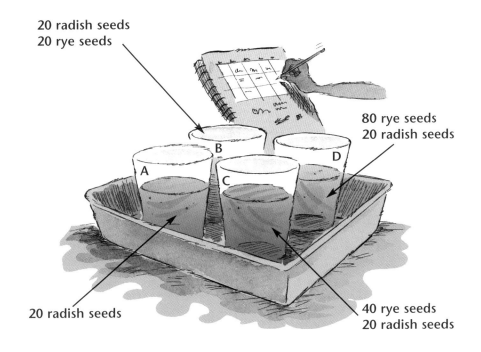

20 radish seeds
20 rye seeds

80 rye seeds
20 radish seeds

B

D

A

C

20 radish seeds

40 rye seeds
20 radish seeds

Plant radish and rye grass seeds in cups.

5. Repeat this process in Week 2 and Week 3. If some of the radish plants die or wilt, make a note in your science notebook.

   How did the germination of radish seeds in CUPS B, C, and D compare with those in CUP A?

Results and Conclusions

Weeds are unwanted plants. Many flower gardeners pull weeds from their flower beds because they may think the weeds are not pretty. But farmers are usually more interested in keeping them from getting into their crops or vegetable gardens because weeds can interfere with the crop yield. Weeds compete with crops or other plants for light, water, nutrients, and other resources. Many times the weeds win and the flowers or crops suffer.

How much do weeds and crops compete? It depends on which weeds are present, the size of the weed population, and the rate at which the weeds grow. Small numbers of weeds can live with cultivated plants without doing any harm. In some situations, weeds can actually help cultivated plants. But if the weed population becomes large, problems arise. Gardeners have to decide when it is time to eliminate the weeds.

In this experiment, you found the point at which weed density becomes great enough to interfere with the growth of radish plants. Did the number of rye grass seeds seem to limit or help the growth of radish seeds in any of the cups? By the end of the experiment, which seedlings were taller in each cup, the radish seedlings or the rye grass seedlings? Were the radish seedlings in all of the cups the same color? Based on your data, do you think that the density of some types of weeds in a garden could limit the growth of wanted plants?

Gardeners often remove invasive weeds from their gardens.

 Science Project Ideas

- Try the experiment again, but this time use seeds other than radishes, such as beans or corn seeds.

- Devise an experiment to find out how weekly removal of unwanted plants affects the growth of desired plants.

- Try an experiment to see how two species of weeds compete against one another.

- Repeat Experiment 3.2, but this time restrict the amount of water available to each cup.

EXPERIMENT 3.3

Out of Sight

Question:

Do microorganisms in the soil influence plant productivity?

Hypothesis:

Microorganisms often help plant productivity.

Materials:

- **an adult**
- 3 empty egg cartons
- bucket
- small scale (a postage stamp or kitchen scale is fine)
- 300 rye grass seeds
- oven
- aluminum baking pan (10-in by 20-in)
- marker
- scissors
- science notebook and pencil
- oven mitt
- hand shovel
- water
- topsoil from garden or forest
- cookie sheet
- 3 paper plates
- ruler
- watch or clock

Procedure:

1. **With the permission of an adult**, turn on the oven to 175°F (80°C).

2. To prepare the three growth containers, cut the tops off three egg cartons. The three tops will be your three grass chambers, so you may throw the bottoms away. With a marker, label the chambers A, B, and C. With a pencil, punch eight small holes in the undersides of the three egg carton tops. These will serve as drainage holes.

3. Using a hand shovel, collect a bucket of topsoil from a garden or a forest. **Ask an adult** to go with you. Pour soil into CHAMBER A until it is level and about one centimeter (½ in) from the top of the chamber. Rake aside a very thin layer of soil and sprinkle 100 rye grass seeds evenly on top of the soil in CHAMBER A. Replace the soil over the seeds so they are completely covered. Set CHAMBER A on one end of a cookie sheet.

4. Pour the rest of the soil from the bucket into a baking pan. By now the oven should have warmed to the proper temperature. **With the help of an adult**, place the pan of soil in the oven. Allow it to heat at 175°F (80°C) for 20 minutes, then **have an adult** use an oven mitt to remove the pan from the oven. The soil is now pasteurized—heated to the point that many, but not all, of the microbes in the soil have been killed. **Ask the adult** to pour some of this soil into CHAMBER B until it is within about one centimeter (½ in) of the top. Set the container of soil aside so it can cool.

5. **With adult help**, change the oven setting to 350°F (176°C). When the oven is ready, **ask the adult** to place the remainder of the soil in the baking pan inside for one hour. At the end of the hour **have the adult** remove the soil, sprinkle it in CHAMBER C, and set it aside while it cools. This soil is sterilized, so all of the microorganisms (both good and bad) have been killed. Turn off the oven.

6. Once soil samples in CHAMBERS B and C have cooled, sprinkle 100 rye grass seeds on each and cover them with soil. Place CHAMBERS B and C on the cookie sheet, next to CHAMBER A. (See Figure 14.)

Figure 14.

Plant rye grass seeds in three different types of soil.

7. When you water your soil and rye seeds, add only enough water to dampen, but not soak, the soil. Be sure to add the same amount of water to each of the three chambers. Place the three chambers in a window so they receive sunlight.

8. Each day for the next four weeks check the soil in each chamber to see if more water is needed. As you add water to one chamber, add it to the other two also.

9. At the end of four weeks, you are ready to harvest your rye grass crop. By now, many of the seeds will have germinated and grown several centimeters tall.

10. Pick up CHAMBER A, a paper plate, and some scissors. Weigh the paper plate on a postage scale and record its weight in your notebook. Use the scissors to clip all the germinated blades of grass from the container. Try to clip them as close to the level of the soil as possible. Place all the clippings on the paper plate. Weigh the paper plate and the clippings and record their combined weight. Subtract the weight of the plate from the weight of the plate plus the clippings. The difference in the two weights represents the biomass of your crop. Record each crop's biomass in your notebook. Dispose of the grass clippings and the paper plate.

11. Repeat the same harvesting and weighing process with CHAMBER B and a new paper plate. Record your findings in your science notebook. Use a third paper plate to collect the clippings from CHAMBER C. Record the weight of these clippings in your notebook. Which container had the heaviest grass clippings? Which had the lightest?

Corn seedlings grow on a farm. Farmers often use pesticides and fertilizers to protect their crops. However, these chemicals destroy microorganisms in the soil.

Results and Conclusions

At first glance, garden soil looks like nothing more than dirt. But productive garden soil is much more. You cannot see them, but millions of tiny microorganisms can be found in good soil. Scientists report that one fourth of a teaspoon of fertile garden soil holds more than 20 million bacteria, 111,000 fungi, and 62,000 algae. Most microorganisms in the soil play roles in decomposing dead matter, converting it into valuable nutrients.

In this experiment, you found out how these microorganisms affect the growth of rye grass. Which soil better supported plant growth with a high biomass of crops? A high biomass of crops is important to farmers.

The greater the crop yield, the better the profit. Many of the chemicals used on large farms, such as pesticides and fertilizers, destroy the microorganisms in soil. On the other hand, organic and sustainable farming uses very few chemicals. Do you think it would be a good idea for farmers to protect microorganisms in the soil?

Based on your results in this experiment, do you think soil microorganisms are important to a plant's growth? Do you think you would be wiser to buy sterilized or pasteurized soil when repotting plants?

 ## Science Project Ideas

- Repeat this experiment with another type of seed. Try growing flowers and finding the biomass of the flower heads.

- Compare the percentage of radish or bean seeds that germinate in pasteurized and sterilized soil. Plant 20 seeds in pasteurized soil and 20 in sterilized soil and find out how many germinate.

- Measure the growth of plants after germination by transplanting some corn seedlings into sterilized soil and into pasteurized soil. Measure the height of the seedlings over time. Watch to see if the leaves of either crop pale in color over time.

EXPERIMENT 3.4

Too Close for Comfort

Question:

How does crowding in a population affect the growth of animals?

Hypothesis:

Crowding limits animal growth.

Materials:

- **an adult**
- about 60 mealworms (from a pet shop or a live bait shop)
- 2 shoeboxes of the same size
- 2 pieces of a small mesh screen (about 10 centimeters by 25 centimeters, or 4 inches by 10 inches)
- piece of large mesh screen (about 40 centimeters by 40 centimeters or 16 inches by 16 inches)
- duct or masking tape
- ruler
- 2 potatoes
- postage scale
- 2 paper plates
- notebook and pencil

continued

continued

- game bird starter (from a feed store) or a mixture of two parts coarsely ground Science Diet Feline Maintenance dry food, one part rolled oats, one part mixed oat and wheat bran, and one part crumbled dry alfalfa
- 2 pieces of newspaper
- knife
- scissors

You will conduct an experiment with mealworms to find out how crowding affects individuals in a population when resources are plentiful. Mealworms are the larval forms of the flour beetle. A flour beetle goes through four stages as it matures: egg, larva, pupa, and beetle. (See Figure 15.) Mature beetles lay eggs that hatch into small larvae. Larvae feed and grow for about six months before they enter the pupa stage. Pupae mature into beetles.

Figure 15.

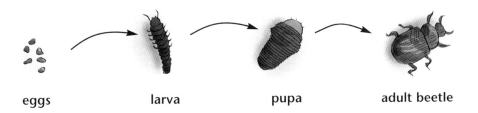

| eggs | larva | pupa | adult beetle |

The flour beetle develops in four stages.

Procedure:

1. You will raise two populations of mealworms in two different shoeboxes. Label one shoebox as A, the control, and the other as B, the experimental. Place enough game bird starter (or your own mixture of food) in each box to cover the bottom to a depth of about 7 ½ centimeters (3 in). Wash and dry two potatoes, then **ask an adult** to cut each into fourths. Place the four cut pieces of one potato in BOX A and the four pieces of the second potato in BOX B. Potatoes provide some moisture for the worms. Loosely cover the game bird starter and potatoes with two or three strips of newspaper, each about the size of the box's interior space. Do not add any water to the contents of the shoeboxes. Water causes the growth of mold that can kill mealworms.

2. Cut an opening that is about 9 centimeters × 24 centimeters (3 ½ × 9 ½ in) in the top of each box so the worms will have plenty of air. To prevent the worms from escaping, cover the hole with fine-mesh screen. Lay the screen on the outside of each box top and tape it in place around the edges.

3. Find the total weight and the average weight of the mealworms. Weigh a paper plate on a postage scale and record its weight in your notebook. Place 10 worms on the paper plate, then weigh the plate and worms. Record this number in your notebook. Now subtract the weight of the plate from the weight of the plate plus the worms to find the weight of all 10 worms. Divide this weight by 10 to find the average weight of each worm. Enter that weight in your notebook. Put these 10 worms under the strips of newspaper and on top of the game bird starter in BOX A. Place the lid on the box. Keep your paper plate for weighing the worms in the future.

4. Repeat the weighing procedure, this time using 50 worms. Find their total weight and average weight and record these numbers in your notebook. Place all 50 worms under the newspaper and on top of the game bird starter in BOX B. Cover BOX B with its lid. Store both boxes in a quiet place at room temperature.

5. After one week, reweigh the worms in each box. To separate the worms in BOX A from their food, gently sift the worms and game bird starter through a piece of large-mesh screen over a large sheet of newspaper. Most of the game bird starter should fall through onto the paper. As it does, carefully collect the worms from the screen. (See Figure 16.)

Figure 16.

To collect the ten mealworms from BOX A, sift the game bird starter through a large-mesh screen.

mealworm   newspaper

Place the worms on the paper plate. (Include any dead worms.) Use the postage scale to find the weight of all ten worms. Calculate their average weight, and record it in your science notebook. Throw out the used game bird starter, which now is mixed with worm feces. Put fresh game bird starter in BOX A. Return the worms, potatoes, and strips of newspaper to BOX A and replace the top. Repeat the procedure with the 50 worms in BOX B.

6. Repeat the weighing procedure again after weeks 2, 3, and 4. As you review your data, what trends do you notice? Are the worms in the crowded box, BOX B, growing at the same rate as the worms in BOX A? Did any of the worms die?

Results and Conclusions

Space is an important factor for living things. Within a population, each individual requires some space. Crowding can affect the health of individuals and their populations.

In your experiment with mealworms, you saw how crowding affects individuals in a population when resources are plentiful. What happened to the worms you observed? How was the population affected? How was the average growth of the worms affected?

When they are extremely crowded, mealworms have been known to start eating each other. What do you think causes this behavior? How is this behavior helpful to the mealworm population as a whole?

Crowding in a mealworm population can affect the worms' growth and health.

Science Project Ideas

- Design an experiment to find out how crowding affects the growth of individuals in a plant population.

- How would you determine how the presence of other species affects the growth of individuals in a mealworm population?

- Do you think that the number of crickets in an ecosystem will limit the number of sow bugs that ecosystem can support? Design an experiment to find out.

EXPERIMENT 3.5

It's a Gas

Question:

Does the presence of ripening fruit affect how fast other fruits ripen?

Hypothesis:

Ripening fruit can trigger other fruits to ripen.

Materials:

- 5 unripe bananas
- 1 ripe banana
- 1 ripe apple
  (or other fruit)
- marker
- 1 ripe tomato
  (or other fruit)
- 4 small brown
  paper bags
- notebook and pencil

Procedure:

1. Create a scale by which you can judge the ripeness of a banana. For example, you could let 5 represent a banana that is so ripe that it is brown and extremely soft. On this same scale, 1 could stand for a green, firm banana. Everything else would fall in between these two numbers.

Figure 17.

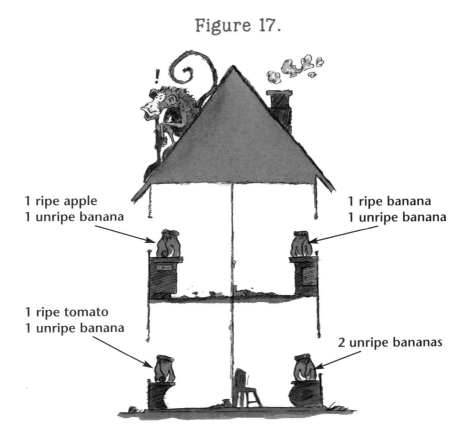

1 ripe apple
1 unripe banana

1 ripe banana
1 unripe banana

1 ripe tomato
1 unripe banana

2 unripe bananas

Place fruit in paper bags.

2. Prepare 4 brown paper bags by labeling them as A, B, C, and D. In BAG A, place a soft, very ripe apple and an unripe banana. In BAG B, place a very ripe banana and an unripe banana. In BAG C, place a very ripe tomato and an unripe banana. With a marker, write 1 on one of the remaining unripe bananas and 2 on the other. Place both in BAG D. (See Figure 17.)

3. Once the fruits are in their proper bags, close and fold down the tops of the bags. The bags cannot be stored together. Place the bags in four different areas of the house. Choose four locations that maintain about the same temperature and receive about the same amount of light.

4. On Day 3, check the fruit inside each of the bags. In BAGS A, B, and C, rate the ripeness of the banana that was originally unripe. In BAG D, rate both pieces of unripe fruit. Enter the results in your science notebook.

5. On Day 6, check the fruit inside the bags once again. In BAGS A, B, and C, rate the ripeness of the banana that was originally unripe. In BAG D, rate both pieces of fruit. Enter your results in your science notebook. Check and rate the ripeness of the fruits again on Day 9.

Results and Conclusions

As some fruits ripen, they produce ethylene gas. Ethylene gas can drift in the air from fruit to fruit, or even from plant to plant. As it travels, it causes the production of chemicals within other fruits. These chemicals trigger the ripening process. With the help of ethylene, the first fruit on a plant can stimulate all the others to ripen. This ensures that the plant will produce plenty of attractive, seed-bearing fruit.

In this experiment, you compared the effectiveness of ethylene from three different sources—bananas, tomatoes, and apples—in stimulating bananas to ripen. Was the ripe apple as effective as the ripe banana in ripening the green banana? How about the ripe tomato? From your observations, can plants of the same type affect each other? How about plants of different types? How would an early ripening fruit tree affect other fruit trees near it?

Science Project Ideas

- Come up with an experiment to show how temperature and light affect the rate of ripening.

- What kind of experiment could you devise that would compare how ripening is affected by different amounts of ethylene gas?

- How could you find out whether birds are more attracted to ripe fruit or to unripe fruit?

- Design an experiment to find out if ethylene given off by a ripe banana affects other fruits (for example, plums, pineapples, and pears).

CHAPTER 4

Humans Affect Ecosystems

Human activities are constantly changing the earth. Since the arrival of humans on the planet, the environment has been altered on several levels: in the atmosphere, in the water, and on the land. Some of the changes are creating serious problems.

One atmospheric problem involves a layer of gases in the upper air, the greenhouse gases, that trap the sun's heat close to the earth. These gases keep the surface of the earth warm. Without any of these gases, the sun's heat would radiate off the earth, leaving the surface very cold. The thickness of this layer of greenhouse gases has been fairly constant for the last several thousand years, producing climates across the earth that fall within a

◀ Many factories and power plants release harmful gasses into the atmosphere.

certain range of high and low temperatures. Some scientists feel that burning fossil fuels in cars and industries has caused the layer to thicken. Many experts believe that as the gas layer grows, it traps more heat, causing the earth's surface to warm more than it has in the past. They believe that this warming has caused a shift in the equilibrium within ecosystems on a global scale. Evidence of these changes includes melting glaciers and an increase in the level of the oceans.

Another air problem concerns a region of ozone gas that protects the earth from dangerous levels of the sun's ultraviolet (UV) radiation. Man-made air pollutants have damaged and thinned this ozone blanket. As a result, more UV radiation is striking the earth now than in the past. High levels of UV radiation can damage living things.

In addition, some of the gases produced by cars and industries have made the rain more acidic. Acid rain is formed when certain air pollutants dissolve in water vapor, then fall to earth. Acid rain damages many forms of life and their environments.

On another front, growth in the human population is stretching water and food supplies to their limits. Many natural underground reservoirs are being drained to provide water for agriculture, industry, and large cities. At the same time, surface water, such as that in rivers, streams, and lakes, is being polluted with chemicals, pesticides, and fertilizers, making the water unfit for use without extensive treatment.

Waterways can be contaminated by hundreds of different pollutants. The sources of water pollutants are grouped into two major categories: point and nonpoint sources. Nonpoint source pollutants are the type that wash into the waterways from many different locations. They include fertilizers from lawns, oils from road surfaces, and salt from irrigation. Point source pollutants are those that enter the water from one particular place. An example of a point source pollutant is the sewage spilling into a river from an overflow pipe at a sewage treatment plant. Poor quality water, along with reduced water supplies, affects the organisms that live in, and depend on, water.

Humans are also changing the landscape. Much of the land that once provided habitats to living things has been converted to farms, residences, industries, or cities. In many places, soil that was once protected by natural plant growth is scraped and exposed by earthmoving equipment. As a result, soil erosion has worsened. Erosion causes the loss of valuable topsoil. It also deposits soil in waterways, where it interferes with the lives of aquatic creatures.

Ecologists are actively looking for solutions to problems that threaten ecosystems. To help solve those problems, they first have to understand them.

EXPERIMENT 4.1

Probing Pollution

Question:

What effects do pollutants have on radish seed germination and root development?

Hypothesis:

Pollution slows or prevents germination and root development.

Materials:

- 30 radish seeds
- aluminum foil
- 3 resealable plastic bags
- measuring cup
- teaspoon
- laundry detergent
- ruler
- 3 jar lids of the same size
- water
- motor oil or vegetable oil
- paper towels
- masking tape
- 3 medicine droppers
- marker
- scissors
- science notebook and pencil

Procedure:

1. Prepare three seed germination chambers from jar lids. Two of the chambers will contain a pollutant and one will not; it serves as the control. With masking tape and a marker, label the three jar lids as A, B, and C. Cut three paper towel circles that will fit snugly inside each jar lid. Place the paper towel disks into the lids.

2. Fill a medicine dropper with water and squirt it gently onto the paper towel in jar LID A until the towel is completely damp. Sprinkle 10 radish seeds on the disk. Make sure that they are evenly spaced.

3. Fill another dropper with motor oil or vegetable oil and gently drop it onto the paper towel in LID B. Use the same quantity of motor oil in LID B as you used water in LID A. Sprinkle 10 radish seeds on the disk, taking care to space them evenly.

4. Mix ½ teaspoon of laundry detergent in ¼ cup of water. Fill a third medicine dropper with the detergent-water mixture then drop it on the paper towel in LID C. Use the same quantity of soapy water as you used water on LID A. Evenly distribute 10 radish seeds on the disk. (See Figure 18.)

5. Wrap each lid in aluminum foil. Be sure to keep the jar lids right-side up. Place the wrapped jar lids in a resealable plastic bag. Set all three jar lids aside for five days.

Figure 18.

Add liquids to each jar lid of seeds.

6. After five days, unwrap and open LID A. Count the number of seeds that germinated. Divide this number by 10, then move the decimal two places to the right to express the number as a percentage. Record this number in your science notebook.

7. With a ruler, measure the lengths of the roots on each seed that germinated. Add the lengths of all the roots and divide by the number of seeds that produced roots to get an average root length. Record this value in your science notebook.

8. Repeat both calculations for seeds in LIDS B and C. Save your germinated seeds for the science project ideas.

Results and Conclusions

Plants and their seeds can be damaged by exposure to pollutants. Seeds are specialized structures that hold and protect embryonic plants. Many plant seeds are tough and resistant to damage, but some are more fragile. Seeds that have been exposed to polluted water may not germinate and develop normally.

In this experiment, you determined the percentage of seeds that germinated in water, water that contains detergents, and water that contains oil. Under what conditions was the percentage of germination the greatest? What conditions caused the roots to grow the longest? Was there a set of conditions in which all seeds failed to germinate? Can you explain why this is so?

Science Project Ideas

- To extend the work you began in this experiment, plant the seeds from each jar lid outdoors or in pots indoors. As plants grow from them, compare their conditions: Are they the same size and color? Do their leaves and stems develop at the same rate?

- Repeat this experiment using other kinds of seeds or water pollutants.

- Devise an experiment to find out how water plants, such as *Elodea* or duckweed, are affected by pollutants.

EXPERIMENT 4.2

No Salt, Please

Question:

How does runoff from salt used to de-ice roads in the winter affect the growth of plants?

Hypothesis:

Salt can hurt plant growth when it enters the soil or the water supply.

Materials:

- **an adult**
- tap water
- soil
- large measuring cup
- de-icing salt (used to melt ice on sidewalks and roads)
- 1 empty 2-liter soda bottle with cap
- 4 empty 1-liter soda bottles with caps

- 4 empty 2-quart plastic containers
- 4 aluminum pie plates
- 40 bean seeds
- nail or ice pick
- marker
- ruler
- string
- tape
- science notebook and pencil

Procedure:

1. Two weeks before you are ready to begin your experiment, plant some bean seeds in four 2-quart plastic containers. Your goal is to grow three bean plants that are 5 centimeters (2 in) tall in each container. To ensure that you have plenty of healthy plants, plant 10 bean seeds in each container.

2. To get started, **have an adult** use a nail or ice pick to punch a few holes in the bottom of four plastic containers. Label the containers A, B, C, and D. Fill each container halfway with soil. Place all four in aluminum pie plates. In each container, plant 10 bean seeds about one centimeter (½ in) deep. Water the seeds so that the soil is moist but no water is standing. Place all of the containers where they will receive sunlight. Check on them daily to see if they need additional water. Add water when the soil feels dry to the touch. (See Figure 19.)

Figure 19.

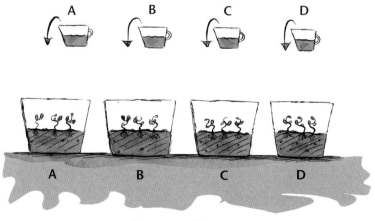

bean seedlings

Grow three bean seedlings in each cup.

3. When you are ready to begin your experiment, take a look at the bean plants in CONTAINER A. Find three seedlings that are about the same size and shape. Gently pull out the other seedlings and throw them away. Loop a small piece of string around each of the remaining plants. With tape, label each string with its own number—1, 2, and 3. Repeat the process with the plants in CONTAINERS B, C, and D.

4. Measure the height of the three plants in CONTAINER A. Enter their heights in your science notebook. Do the same for the plants in CONTAINERS B, C, and D.

5. Prepare a starting salt solution in a 2-liter bottle. You will use this to help you make three of your four experimental solutions: a strong solution, a moderate solution, and a weak solution. First, put 9 ⅓ tablespoons (about 200 g) of salt in the 2-liter bottle, then fill the bottle almost completely with water. Cap the bottle and shake it to dissolve the salt. This is your starting salt solution. (See Figure 20.)

Figure 20.

Prepare the watering solutions.

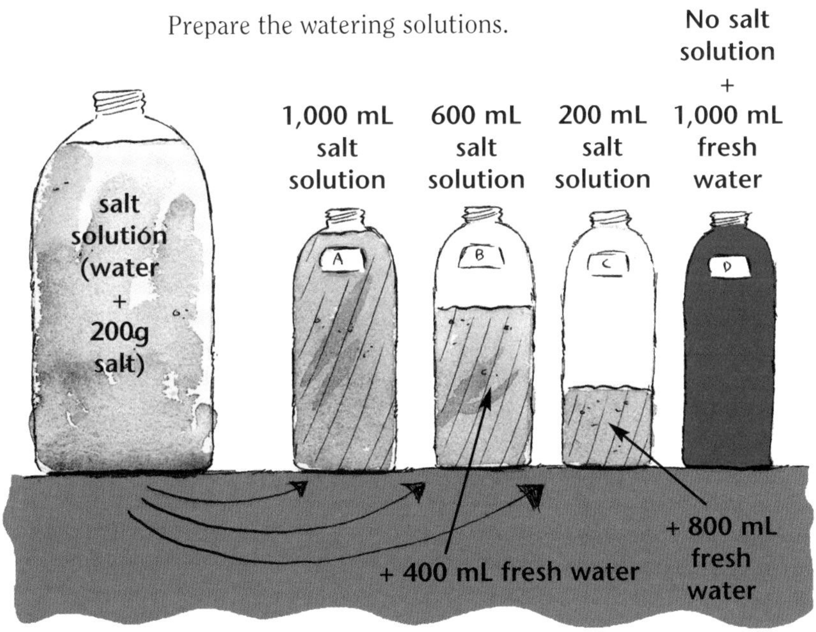

No salt
solution
+

1,000 mL   600 mL   200 mL   1,000 mL
salt   salt   salt   fresh
solution   solution   solution   water

salt
solution
(water
+
200g
salt)

A   B   C   D

+ 800 mL
fresh
water

+ 400 mL fresh water

6. Label the first 1-liter bottle as SOLUTION A, the second as SOLUTION B, the third as SOLUTION C, and the fourth as D—NO SALT. Pour 1,000 milliliters (about one qt) of the starting salt solution into a large measuring cup. Transfer this to the SOLUTION A bottle. SOLUTION A is the strong salt solution.

7. To prepare SOLUTION B, the moderate saltwater solution, measure out 600 milliliters (about ½ qt) of the starting salt solution and transfer it to the bottle labeled SOLUTION B. Now measure 400 milliliters (about ⅓ qt) of tap water and add it to the bottle. Place the cap on the bottle and shake.

8. To prepare SOLUTION C, the weak saltwater solution, measure 200 milliliters (about ¼ qt) of starting salt solution into a measuring cup, then transfer it to the bottle labeled SOLUTION C. Add 800 milliliters (about ⅔ qt) of tap water to the bottle labeled SOLUTION C. Place the cap on the bottle and shake.

9. Thoroughly rinse the measuring cup, then collect 1,000 milliliters (about one qt) of tap water and pour it into the bottle labeled D—NO SALT. This represents fresh water.

10. Check on the plants daily for the next two weeks to see if they need watering with their corresponding solution. Remember that if you water one plant with its experimental solution, you must give an equal amount to the plants in the other containers of their solutions. Try to adjust your watering so that the soil in each container is damp but not soggy.

11. Every other day, use your ruler to find the height of each bean plant. Enter their heights in your notebook. Also observe the color and condition of the leaves. If leaves change color, make a note about that in your science notebook. Leaves may change from green to yellow, pale green, or brown. Leaves may also show some browning around the edges. If so, note it in your science notebook. Make observations every other day for two weeks.

Results and Conclusions

When temperatures are low, people in some areas of the country find themselves traveling on highways that are covered by dangerously slick ice. To remove the ice, many communities spread salt on the roads. Salt water has a lower freezing point than freshwater, so it remains a liquid even when temperatures are below freezing.

Even though salt on an icy road is helpful to motorists, it can spell disaster for the plants living nearby. When the salt water runs off the roadway, it covers the roots of plants, often damaging them. Even plants that are not in the path of runoff suffer from the effects of salty spray and mist that splashes on their leaves. Sodium chloride and other salts are known to stunt growth, cause parts of the plants to die, and damage buds in the tops of plants.

In this experiment, you determined the effects of three different concentrations of salt water on plants. Which concentration allowed the bean plants to grow tallest? Which caused the bean plants to change color? Did any of the plants show browning around the edges? If so, which ones? Did any of the plants wilt or die? How do you think the concentration of salt in the solutions affected the growth of your bean plants?

 Science Project Ideas

- In the winter, when roads are de-iced, some plants are "showered" in salty water. To find out how salt mist affects plant growth, repeat this experiment, but water all of the plants with regular tap water. Mist the plants with different solutions of salt water and observe the results.

- In some places, calcium chloride (rock salt) is used instead of sodium chloride. Set up an experiment to test the impact of calcium chloride runoff on plant growth.

- Come up with a method of testing how salt affects the ability of seeds to germinate.

- Most roadsides are sown with grasses. Devise an experiment to find out which kinds of grasses are most tolerant of salt.

EXPERIMENT 4.3

Acid Bath

Question:

Does the acidity of water affect the production of new roots in plants?

Hypothesis:

Water acidity stunts the production of new roots.

Materials:

- 4 cups or small jars
- pH paper, garden soil pH test kit, or pH meter (from garden shop)
- baking soda
- vinegar
- bottled distilled water
- two 2-cup measuring cups
- stirring spoon
- masking tape
- teaspoon
- scissors
- marker
- ruler
- coleus or begonia plant (from garden shop)
- philodendron plant (from garden shop)
- science notebook and pencil

Procedure:

1. Label your four cups or jars with a marker. Write the word ACID on two cups and the word WATER on the other two cups.

   Prepare an acidic growing solution. For this, you will use vinegar, which is a weak acid. In a measuring cup, mix one teaspoon of vinegar in 2 cups of distilled water and stir well. Check the pH of the water in one of three ways: either dip one end of a piece of pH paper in the water, use a garden soil pH test kit, or check with a pH meter. No matter how you test the pH, it should be about 4. If it is lower than 4, add ⅛ teaspoon of baking soda, stir, and test again. Baking soda is a base and it raises the pH of a solution. If the pH is above 4, add about ⅛ of a teaspoon of vinegar and test with pH paper again. Keep adjusting until you end up with a pH of 4. Divide the solution between the two cups labeled ACID.

2. In the second measuring cup, pour 2 cups of distilled water. Check the pH of the distilled water. The pH should be about 6, which is slightly acidic, like rainwater. If necessary, adjust the pH as you did in the previous step, adding baking soda or vinegar as needed. Divide the solution between the two cups labeled WATER.

3. To prepare your plant cuttings, select a stem of begonia or coleus. With scissors, cut the stem into several sections. Make certain that each section includes one leaf and at least 10 centimeters (4 in) of stem. (See Figure 21.) Prepare six begonia or coleus cuttings. Next, select a stem of philodendron and cut it the same way so that you have six philodendron cuttings.

4. Place three coleus or begonia cuttings in one of the cups labeled ACID, and the other three in one of the cups labeled WATER. In the second cup labeled ACID, place three philodendron cuttings, and put the last three philodendron cuttings in the other cup labeled WATER. Place all four cups in an area where they will receive some light.

Figure 21.

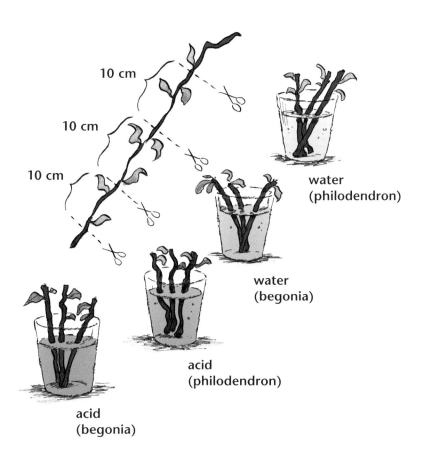

Prepare cuttings of plants. Dotted lines represent places to cut.

5. Every few days, check on the plants to make sure that their stems are still submerged in liquid. Add the appropriate liquid to each cup as it evaporates.

6. After 7 days, examine the submerged ends of each cutting for new root growth. Young roots will look like knobs, hairs, or tiny branches forming on the stem. Record the number of roots that are appearing on each stem.

7. After another 7 days, check the cuttings again. In your notebook, record the number of additional roots appearing on each stem.

Results and Conclusions

It seems natural to think of rainwater as pure and clean. However, pollutants in the air can dissolve in water vapor to form acids. Acid precipitation in the form of rain, snow, or sleet can damage the environment. You have probably heard the term "acid rain."

Acidity is measured on the pH scale, which extends from 1 to 14. Materials that are neutral, neither acid nor base, have a pH of 7. Acids have pHs between 0 and 7, slightly acid water has a pH of 6, and very acidic solutions have a pH of 1. Substances that are bases have pHs between 7 and 14.

In this experiment, you saw how the pH of water affects the production of new roots on plants. What were your results? Did all of the plant cuttings develop roots? Did they develop them at the same rate? Does acidity seem to affect root development? Why do you think that two types of plants were used in this experiment?

Science Project Ideas

- With the help of an adult, prepare acid solutions (using distilled water and muriatic acid, which is sold in stores that carry building and pool supplies) with pHs of 2 and 3 to find out how extremely acidic conditions affect root production.

- With the help of an adult, prepare strong basic solutions (using distilled water and ammonia) with pHs of 8 to 10 to find out how very basic conditions affect root production.

- Collect some rainwater and water from local ponds, creeks, lakes, and rivers. Check the acidity of each. Devise an experiment to test how each water sample affects root growth.

- Think of an experiment to test the effects of acid rain on the leaves of plants.

- Create an experiment that can test how acid rain affects germination of seeds.

EXPERIMENT 4.4

Shrimp Forecast: Clear to Partly Cloudy

Question:

How does cloudy water from soil runoff affect the growth of animals in an aquatic environment?

Hypothesis:

Cloudy water can stunt the growth of aquatic animals.

Materials:

- two 2-liter soda bottles
- scissors
- marker
- teaspoon
- tablespoon
- water
- table salt (that does not contain iodine)
- brine shrimp eggs (from pet store)
- magnifying glass
- spoon
- soil (clay or silt works best; do not use potting soil)
- 2 aquarium pumps
- plastic tubing
- baker's yeast
- science notebook and pencil
- saucer
- medicine dropper
- white paper
- masking tape

Procedure:

1. On Day 1, about 48 hours before you are ready to start your experiment, prepare two saltwater tanks for your brine shrimp. Brine shrimp are tiny, saltwater animals that are similar to many of the species that live in fresh-water ecosystems. Cut away the top third of two 2-liter soda bottles and recycle them; you will only use the bottom portion of each bottle. Rinse the bottles well, then fill each about half full of tap water. With tape and a marker, label one as TANK A and the other as TANK B.

2. Measure out one tablespoon of salt and stir it into the water in TANK A. Repeat this procedure for TANK B. TANK A will act as the control, and B will be your experimental tank.

3. To keep normal levels of oxygen in the tanks, they will need to be aerated. Insert one end of a length of plastic tubing into the water of TANK A and attach the other end to a small aquarium pump. Do the same for TANK B. Turn on the pumps so that they gently aerate the two saltwater tanks. (See Figure 22.)

4. To TANK B, add 4 tablespoons of soil and stir gently. If you can still see through the bottle of water, add more soil. The addition of soil makes the water cloudier, or more turbid. Add soil until the water is cloudy. Several times a day, gently stir the water in TANK B to keep the soil suspended in water.

5. Examine some dry brine shrimp eggs, which you can purchase from a pet store. Sprinkle a few onto a piece of white paper, and look at them closely with a magnifying glass. In your notebook, draw a sketch of two or three dried eggs.

6. The next day, on Day 2, start your cultures of brine shrimp. Measure half a teaspoon of eggs and sprinkle them into TANK A.

Figure 22.

tap water
with iodine

Prepare saltwater tanks for brine shrimp.

7. Repeat the procedure for TANK B. The eggs of brine shrimp are actually embryos within thin shells. As long as brine shrimp eggs are kept dry, the embryos within them remain inactive. However, once they are placed in salt water, they become active. After about 22 hours in room-temperature salt water, the eggs burst open and the embryos slowly emerge. As they grow, the young shrimp shed their tough outer skins several times. Eventually, they will reach the mature length of 10 to 20 millimeters ($\frac{1}{3}$ to $\frac{3}{4}$ inches).

8. Prepare food for your brine shrimp by mixing one fourth of a teaspoon of baker's yeast with a little salt water. After Day 3, you can feed your shrimp with a medicine dropper by adding a few drops of the milky solution to each of the bottles. Be careful not to overfeed because young brine shrimp are not big eaters. Store the unused yeast solution in a plastic container in the refrigerator.

9. On Day 3, gently stir the water in TANK A. Then take a sample of water from the tank with your medicine dropper. Place the sample in a saucer and examine it with your magnifying glass. Record the number of moving brine shrimp that you can see. Return the shrimp to their tank. Rinse the dropper and repeat the counting activity with TANK B.

10. Take samples of brine shrimp from each tank and count the organisms in the samples on days four, five, and six. Each day, enter your results into your notebook.

Results and Conclusions

Living things are affected by any changes in their ecosystem. If soil washes into a stream, it can increase the turbidity, or cloudiness, of the water. Soil can be loosened around streams by a lot of human activities, including construction, logging of forests, over-grazing of pastures, and cultivation of crops.

Increased turbidity can harm the entire aquatic ecosystem. Suspended particles prevent sunlight from filtering through. When light is low, the rate of photosynthesis in plants and green algae slows and plants cannot make as much food as they normally would. Plants serve as the basis for many food chains in a water ecosystem. In addition, reduced photosynthesis means less oxygen in the water for animals.

Turbidity causes other problems. Dirt in streams and ponds can clog the feeding structures of many small animals. The combination of reduced levels of oxygen and clogged feeding structures make it very hard for some animals to survive.

In this experiment, you determined if an increase in water turbidity affects the rate at which brine shrimp mature. Were you able to see a difference in the two populations of brine shrimp you observed? Were there more shrimp living in the clear or turbid water? Why do you think this is so? Were the shrimp in both tanks about the same size? Were any of the shrimp dead? If so, were there more dead shrimp in TANK A or B?

Science Project Ideas

- Test the growth of other organisms in cloudy and clear aquatic environments. See how turbidity affects the growth of water plants, such as *Elodea* and duckweed.

- How does turbidity affect the temperature of water over a period of two weeks?

- Devise a way to measure turbidity in local waterways, then keep a journal of turbidity levels over time.

- How would turbidity affect minnows in a pond? Set up an experiment to test your hypothesis.

EXPERIMENT 4.5

Packed Tight

Question:

How does soil compaction from human travel impact the levels of water and oxygen in that soil?

Hypothesis:

Human travel decreases the levels of water and oxygen in soil.

Materials:

- **an adult**
- long nail or ice pick
- ruler
- large tin can (16 or 32 ounces) with ends and label removed
- pitcher of water
- watch with a second hand
- science notebook and pencil
- hand shovel (optional)
- plant identification guide

Procedure:

1. Select four different soil sites in your neighborhood or schoolyard. Site A should be a place where human travel is heavy, Site B a location where human travel is moderate, Site C where little human traffic occurs, and Site D an area that gets no human traffic. Do not trespass on, or take samples from, someone's yard without permission, and take **an adult** with you.

2. Visit Site A and record its location. In your notebook, make a note of the number of different kinds of plants and animals at Site A. First, check out how many kinds of plants you see growing on the surface of the soil, as well as evidence of different plants from other places (such as dead leaves or twigs). Refer to a plant identification guide for help in distinguishing different species. Also write down how many different animals you see, as well as evidence of animals (such as a gnawed pinecone or droppings). Finally, dig down a few inches and inspect the soil for evidence of plant or animal life (such as roots, seeds, or worms).

3. Brush any leaf litter from the top of the soil sample. Push the long nail or ice pick into the soil as far as possible. The nail will not be able to penetrate compacted soil as easily as it can penetrate noncompacted soil. Remove the nail and measure how many centimeters it penetrated into the soil. Record this value into your notebook.

4. Next, measure how fast water seeps into the soil. Areas that are highly compacted may not be able to absorb water as quickly as less compacted areas. Reduced water absorption can limit the number and kinds of organisms that live in soil. Take a tin can from which the ends and label have been removed. Firmly push the can into the soil to a depth of 2 or 3 centimeters (0.8 to 1.1 inches). Fill the can with water, then time how long it takes for the water to drain from the can into the soil. (See Figure 23.) Record this time in your notebook.

5. Repeat the entire process at sites B, C, and D. Record your results in your science notebook.

Results and Conclusions

In this experiment, you compared the productivity of soil that is loosely packed to that of soil that is tightly packed by looking at the number of plant and animal species living in each. At which of the four sites that you examined did you find the most kinds of plants? At which did you find the most kinds of animals? In which site did water drain into soil

Figure 23.

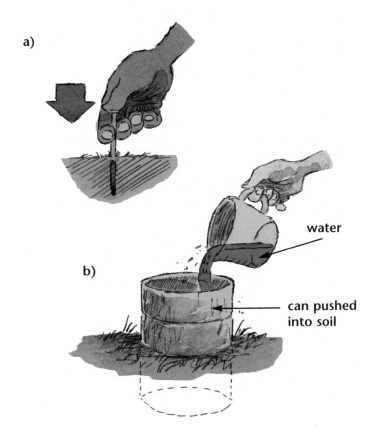

a)

b)

water

can pushed
into soil

To test how compacted the soil is, you can
(a) push a nail into the surface and
(b) watch how quickly water seeps into the soil. Measure how long
it takes for water to seep from the can.

the fastest? At which site was it most difficult to push the nail into the soil? From this experiment, can you make a statement about how soil compaction affects the plant and animal life in an area?

The texture and amount of air spaces between soil particles is important to plant and animal life in an ecosystem. The growth of some plants can be slowed by highly compacted soil. That is why before they do any planting, farmers and gardeners take time to break up tightly packed soil. By loosening soil, they make it easier for water and oxygen to get to plant roots. Landscapers aerate lawns for the same reason. People who raise earthworms also make sure that soil particles are loose and well aerated to support the worm population.

When they are preparing an area to be planted, farmers, gardeners, and landscapers may caution people not to walk over the loosened soil. Walking and driving over these areas presses the soil particles closer together, compacting them. Certain soils, such as clay, tend to compact more tightly than others, such as sand. When soil becomes compacted, water seeps through it slowly and little oxygen can work its way down to plant roots.

Science Project Ideas

- Expand this experiment and find out if compacted soil or soil that is not compacted is more prone to erosion.

- Design and perform an experiment that shows which type of soil—sand, loam, clay, or silt—is most likely to experience compaction.

- Earthworms require loosely spaced areas between soil particles. How could you verify this experimentally?

- Create an experiment that determines the effect of compacted soil on seed germination. Can you use the results of this experiment to explain why forest rangers ask hikers to stay on the trails in state parks?

Appendix

SCIENCE SUPPLY COMPANIES

Aldon Corporation
1533 West Henrietta Road
Avon, NY 14414-9409
800-724-9877
http://www.aldon-chem.com

Becker Underwood
1305 South 58th Street
Saint Joseph, MO 64507
800-232-5907
http://www.beckerunderwood.com/

Carolina Biological Supply Company
2700 York Road
Burlington, NC 27215
800-334-5551
http://www.carolina.com

**Connecticut Valley Biological
  Supply Company**
82 Valley Road
South Hampton, MA 01703
800-355-6813
http://www.ctvalleybio.com

Delta Education
80 Northwest Boulevard
P.O. Box 3000
Nashua, NH 03061-3000
(800) 258-1302
http://www.delta-education.com/

Discovery Scope® Inc
3202 Echo Mountain Drive
Kingwood, TX 77345
http://www.discoveryscope.com

Edmund Scientific
60 Pearce Avenue
Tonawanda, NY 14150
800-728-6999
http://www.scientificsonline.com

Fisher Science Education
485 South Frontage Road
Burr Ridge, IL 60521
800-955-1177
http://www.fisheredu.com

Flinn Scientific
P.O. Box 219
Batavia, IL 60510-0219
800-452-1261
http://www.flinnsci.com

Frey Scientific
80 Northwest Boulevard
Nashua, NH 03063
(800) 225-3739
http://www.freyscientific.com/

Neo/SCI Corporation
P.O. Box 22729
100 Aviation Avenue
Rochester, NY 14692-2729
800-526-6689
http://www.neosci.com

Science Kit and Boreal Laboratories
777 East Park Drive
P.O. Box 5003
Tonawanda, NY 14151-5003
(800) 828-7777
http://sciencekit.com

Glossary

acid rain—Precipitation that results when pollutants
   from the air dissolve in water vapor.

adaptation—A structural or behavioral feature that
   helps a living thing survive.

allelopathic plants—Plants that release chemicals to
   keep other plants from growing close to them.

Berlese funnel—A device in which soil is placed so that
   light can be applied from above to force invertebrates
   into a collection jar.

biodiversity—The variety of living things in an
   ecosystem.

biomass—The weight of living matter in a community
   or ecosystem.

chlorophyll—The green pigment in plants that absorbs
   the sun's energy.

climate—The weather conditions in a place over a
   period of time.

cold-blooded—A word that describes an animal whose
   body temperature is influenced by the temperature of
   the environment.

commensalism—A relationship between two different
   kinds of animals in which one of the organism benefits,
   but the other organism is neither helped nor harmed.

consumers—Animals that take in energy by eating
   plants or plant-eating animals.

decomposers—Organisms that break down complex materials into simpler ones, taking energy for themselves and releasing nutrients back into the soil.

ecology—The study of relationships between living things and their environment.

ecosystem—An organization of all living things and nonliving things that interact with each other.

ecotone—The area where two ecosystems merge.

erosion—The wearing away of rock or soil by wind, water, or chemicals.

ethylene gas—A gas that is produced by fruit and that triggers ripening.

evaporation—The process in which a liquid changes to a gas.

fauna—All of the animals in an ecosystem.

fermentation—The process of converting food into energy without oxygen. By-products of fermentation include carbon dioxide gas and alcohol.

food chain—An arrangement of who eats whom in an ecosystem. A food chain traces the path of energy through that system.

fossil fuels—The remains of plants and animals that have been geologically changed to oil, gas, and coal.

fruit—The enlarged, sweetened ovary of a plant.

germination—The growth of a young plant from its seed.

gill—The respiratory organ found in many aquatic animals.

greenhouse gases—A group of gases in the atmosphere, including carbon dioxide, methane, and water vapor, that transmit the sun's energy to earth, but prevent the escape of heat from the earth's surface.

guard cells—Cells on either side of a leaf's stoma that open and close the stoma.

hypothesis—An idea that can be experimentally tested, or an educated guess about the outcome of an experiment.

invertebrates—Animals without backbones.

litter—Dead plant material lying on top of the soil.

mutualism—A relationship in which two organisms live together to the benefit of both.

nonpoint source pollutants—Pollutants that wash into the waterways from many different locations.

ozone—A form of oxygen in the upper atmosphere that can absorb ultraviolet light.

parasitism—A relationship between two organisms, in which one member is harmed and the other benefits.

pH scale—A measure of acidity ranging from 1 to 14. Acids have pHs that range between 0 and 7; bases have pHs between 7 and 14.

photosynthesis—The process of capturing the sun's energy to turn it into the sugar that plants need to live.

point source pollutants—Pollutants that enter the water from one particular place.

population—A large group of the same kind of organisms in an ecosystem.

predator—An animal that eats other animals for food.

prey—An animal that is eaten by other animals for food.

producers—Organisms that contain chlorophyll and can capture the sun's energy. They are the beginning of the food chain.

respiration—A process that occurs in the presence of oxygen that converts food into energy that cells use to carry out life processes.

roots—Plant organs that absorb nutrients and water and anchor a plant in the ground.

runoff—Rainwater that is not absorbed by soil.

stoma—Tiny hole in plant leaves that determines the rate of transpiration.

succession—The process in which one type of ecosystem slowly changes into a different type of ecosystem.

topsoil—The rich, uppermost layer of soil.

transpiration—The loss of water from the stoma of plant's leaves due to evaporation.

turbidity—A measure of the cloudiness of water.

UV (ultraviolet) light—High-energy form of light just beyond violet on the electromagnetic spectrum.

warm-blooded—An animal that can maintain a constant body temperature through its metabolic processes.

Further Reading

Bochinski, Julianne Blair. *The Complete Workbook for Science Fair Projects*. Hoboken, N.J.: Wiley, 2005.

Cherry, Lynne and Gary Braasch. *How We Know What We Know About Our Changing Climate: Scientists and Kids Explore Global Warming*. Nevada City, CA: Dawn Publications, 2008.

Haduch, Bill. *Science Fair Success Secrets: How to Win Prizes, Have Fun, and Think Like a Scientist*. New York: Dutton Children's Books, 2002.

MacMillan, Dianne M. *Life in a Deciduous Forest*. Minneapolis, Minn.: Lerner, 2004.

Reilly, Kathleen M. *Planet Earth: 25 Environmental Projects You Can Build Yourself*. White River Junction, Vt.: Nomad Press, 2008.

Richardson, Gillian. *Ecosystems: Science Q & A*. New York, NY: Weigl Publishers, 2009.

Van Vleet, Carmella. *Amazing Arctic & Antarctic Projects You Can Build Yourself*. White River Junction, VT. Nomad Press, 2008.

Vecchione, Glen. *Blue Ribbon Science Projects*. New York: Sterling Pub. Co., 2005.

Vickers, Tanya M. *Teen Science Fair Sourcebook: Winning School Science Fairs and National Competitions*. Enslow Publishers, Inc., 2009.

Internet Addresses

Department of Ecology, Environmental Ed Home.
Access Washington. "Just for Kids."
<http://www.ecy.wa.gov/services/ee/kids.html>

Los Angeles County Office of Education. "Fast Plants
Student Activities."
<http://teams.lacoe.edu/documentation/classrooms/
gary/plants/plants.html>

National Center for Ecological Analysis and Synthesis.
"Kids Do Ecology." 2001.
<http://www.nceas.ucsb.edu/nceas-web/kids/>

Index

A

acid rain, 118, 134–135
acids, 131–134
adaptations, 28–29, 37, 38
alfalfa seeds, 90–94
algae, 87, 89, 104
allelopathic chemicals, 93
allelopathic plants, 93–94
animal
    classification groups, 54
    evidence, 47
    shelters, 35–38
animal species diversity, 45–50

B

baker's yeast, 70, 74, 136, 139
bases, 134
bean seed, 125–130
behavioral adaptation, 29
Berlese funnel, 52, 54–55
biodiversity, 33, 49, 50
biomass, 103–105
black walnut trees, 93, 94

bread mold, 75
brine shrimp, 136, 137
    effect of water turbidity on
        maturity rate, 137–140
    eggs, 139

C

carbon dioxide, 28, 60, 73, 74
castings, 84
chlorophyll, 28
classifying organisms into
    groups, 54–57
climate, 27, 29, 35–37, 59, 117
cold-blooded animals, 79
commensalism, 89
consumers, 28, 60
crickets, 40, 47, 111
crowding, 106–111

D

data, 15–16
data table, 13
decomposers, 28, 60, 87
desert ecosystems, 27, 28, 31

detergent, 120–123
distilled water, 132–135
    checking pH of, 132

E

earthworms, 81–85, 146–147
    and light intensity, 81–85
ecologists, 27, 29, 49, 60, 119
ecology, 27
ecosystems, 7, 146
    characteristics of, 27–29
    defined, 27
ecotone, 31, 33, 34
effects of sunlight, 39–44
    impact of human activity,
        117–119
    and living factors, 87–89
    neighboring and overlapping,
        30–34
    and nonliving factors, 59–60
    and species diversity, 45–49
Elodea, 124, 141
embryo, 63, 139
energy, 28, 43, 60
erosion, 119, 147
ethylene gas, 114
    and the fruit ripening
        process, 114–115

evaporation, 60
experiment design, 15

F

fauna, 56–57
fermentation, 70, 71–75
fertilizers, 105, 118, 119
flour beetle, 107
food chain, 28, 140
forest ecosystems, 27, 33
fossil fuels, 118
freshwater ecosystem, 137
fruit, 112–115
fungi, 28, 29, 50, 73, 74, 87, 89,
        104

G

germination, 63, 91, 93, 94, 96,
        97, 120–123, 147
    effects of pollution, 120–124
    role of water, 61–64
germination rate, 92–93
goldfish, 77
    influence of temperature
        change on breathing rate,
        76–80
greenhouse gases, 117–118
guard cells, 68–69

H

human impact
    on ecosystems, 117–119
    on levels of water and oxygen
        in soil, 142–146
hypothesis, 14

I

insects, 40, 54
invertebrates, 52, 54, 56, 57

L

larvae, 54, 107
lichens, 29, 87, 88–89
light
    effect on earthworm
        behavior, 81–85
    energy, 60
    impact on organisms living
        in ecosystems, 31–49,
        78–79
    intensity, 81–85
litter, 52–57, 144

M

mealworms, 106–108
    effect of crowding on
        population, 106–111

microorganisms, 104
    effect on rye grass growth,
        101–104
migration, 29
moisture, 59–60
mold, 42, 43, 73, 75, 108
mutualism, 88

N

nonliving factors of ecosystems,
    59–60
nutrients, 28, 29, 60, 104

O

oil, 119, 120–123
oxygen, 28, 29, 73, 77, 137,
    140, 142, 146
ozone gas, 118

P

parasitism, 89
pasteurized soil, 101–105
pH scale, 132
pH of water
    effect on new root growth of
        plants, 132–135
    methods of checking, 132
photosynthesis, 28, 140

plant species diversity, 45,
    46–49, 50
pollutants
    acidity, 134–135
    contaminating waterways,
        119
    effect on radish seed
        germination and root
        development, 120–124
    effect of salt water on plants,
        125–130
    nonpoint source, 119
point source, 119
pond ecosystem, 29, 31
population, 27–29, 31, 88
    effect of crowding on,
        106–111
predator and prey relationships,
    87–88
producers, 28, 63, 87

R

radish seeds, 61–63, 90–93,
    95–98, 121
rainfall, 29
rainwater, 132, 134, 135
rate of fermentation, 73, 74, 75
rate of transpiration, 68, 69

reservoir, 59, 118
respiration, 28, 73, 76–78
ripening fruit, 114
    effect on how fast other
        fruit ripens, 114–115
roots, 68, 131–134, 143, 146
rye grass seeds, 95–98,
    100–104

S

safety, 24–25
salt, 119, 129
saltwater
    effect on plants, 125–130
    runoff, 129
scat, 47
science fair report, 16–19
science fair tips, 21–23
science fairs, 20–21
science projects, 8–9
scientific method, 12–13
seeds
    development of, 114
    germination of, 61–64, 99,
        102–103, 105, 120–123
shelter, 35–38
snails and slugs, 54
sodium chloride, 125–130

soil, 56
  characteristics, 60
  comparing animal life in
    field and forest, 51–57
  comparing garden and forest,
    101–105
  erosion, 119
  pasteurized, 101–105
  sterilized, 102, 105
  and turbidity, 140–141
soil particles
  aerated, 137, 146
  comparing productivity of,
    142–146
  highly compacted, 146
sowbug, 85, 111
space, 90–94
stoma, 68–69
stream ecosystem, 27
structural adaptations, 28
succession, 29
sugar, 28, 71, 72, 75

T

temperature, 59
  effect on breathing rate
    of goldfish, 76–80
  effect on rate of
    fermentation, 70–75

topsoil, 56, 57, 119
topsoil ecosystems, 52–57
transpiration, 65–69
tundra, 36–38
turbidity, 140
  effect on maturity rate of
    brine shrimp, 137–140
  problems caused by, 140, 141

U

ultraviolet (UV) radiation, 118

W

warm-blooded animals, 78–79
water cycle, 59–60
water pollutants, 119
weed density, 95–99
weeds, 95–99
worms, 54

Y

yeast, 74, 136, 139
  fermentation, 71–75